THE CYPRIA

Works by D. M. Smith

Munley Priory: A Gothic Story
The Cypria: Reconstructing the Lost Prequel to Homer's Iliad
The Telegony: Rediscovering the Lost Epilogue to Homer's Odyssey

The Troy Myth in Medieval Britain

I. John Lydgate's Troy Book: A Middle English Iliad
II. The Seege of Troye & The Rawlinson Prose Siege of Troy
III. The Laud Troy Book: The Forgotten Troy Romance

*RECONSTRUCTING THE LOST PREQUEL
TO HOMER'S ILIAD:*

THE CYPRIA

EDITED & WITH INTRODUCTION BY
D. M. SMITH

ISBN: 9781546302957

To Ingri & Edgar Parin d'Aulaire,
for capturing a young imagination

CONTENTS

INTRODUCTION

IT IS generally known that Homer's *Iliad* and *Odyssey* did not always exist in isolation. The *Iliad* begins with the Trojan War already in its tenth year, and ends with walls of Ilium still standing and the doomed Achilles still very much alive. By the time the *Odyssey* picks up the tale the war has ended, with only its titular hero yet to return home. In Classical times there were no such gaps in the narrative, the enclosing and intervening episodes of the war having been taken up by other poets, forming a "cycle" of epic poems of which only Homer's contributions survive to the present day.

These eight poems are collectively known as the "Epic Cycle", although that term more commonly refers to the six epics not authored by Homer—even in antiquity "Cyclic" was distinct from "Homeric". The *Cypria* described the early years of the war, from the very seeds of the conflict in the wedding of Peleus and Thetis, to the rape of Helen, the marshalling of the Greek armies, and the initial invasion of the Troad. Homer's *Iliad* is centred around the quarrel of Agamemnon and Achilles, and the latter's slaying of Hector, while the *Aethiopis* continued the story with the introduction of the Trojans' Amazonian and Aethiopian allies, and the death of Achilles. The *Little Iliad* told the story of the contest for Achilles' arms and the arrival of his son Neoptolemus, the death of Paris, and the building of the wooden horse. *Iliou Persis* focused on the sack of Troy, and *Nostoi* the various misadventures of the departing Greeks—excluding Odysseus of course, whose homecoming was afforded an epic of its own. The *Odyssey* was followed by the *Telegony*, which concluded the cycle with the death of Odysseus at the hands of Telegonus, his estranged son by the goddess Circe.*

The non-Homeric epics are believed to date from the 7th century BC—roughly a century after the composition of the *Iliad* and *Odyssey*—although it is not strictly correct to view them as later works. A distinction must be made between the creation of these myths and their transition from an oral tradition to a written text. The narrative as a whole undoubtedly existed long before the various episodes were first written down, and the Homeric poems clearly assume a certain knowledge of the wider story. If considered as a semi-mythical history of the Greek Bronze Age (the fall of Troy, supposing the legend does indeed have an historical precedent, is tentatively placed at around 1200 BC), this collection of tales may well have developed over a period of several centuries—even as they have continued to evolve in the three millennia since.

This notion of the Epic Cycle developing organically through oral transmission challenges the traditional view of these poems as representing the work of

---

* Some scholars (both ancient and modern) include the *Titanomachy* and the four poems of the Theban Cycle, the *Oedipodia*, *Thebaid*, *Epigoni* and *Alcmeonis*, bringing the total to thirteen. This "Greater Epic Cycle" would have begun with the overthrow of Cronus and the Titans, then the story of Oedipus, the Seven Against Thebes, and their sons the Epigoni—most of whom went on to fight at Troy. This extended list remains controversial, and for the purpose of this volume I refer only to those poems pertaining to the Trojan War.

individual authors; perhaps rendering moot an argument almost as old as the epics themselves. The so-called "Oral Theory" gained mainstream acceptance in the 20th century through the work of Milman Parry and Albert Lord, although its roots go back three hundred years earlier, when the existence of Homer—once sacrosanct—first began to be questioned. It may be that those historically named as authors earned this distinction by virtue of being the first to commit these epics to papyrus. In any case it is impossible to definitively link any one poem to a particular author; today even the *Iliad* and *Odyssey* are commonly accepted as being the work of two different poets.

Jonathan S. Burgess suggests that the Epic Cycle was not originally conceived as a cohesive unit. Rather than the result of a collection of poets writing in response to one another, the Cycle may have been "manufactured" during the Hellenistic period (323 to 31 BC) by stitching together several ancient and completely independent epics in chronological order, omitting entire books where the narratives overlapped. These truncated epics then assumed a canonical status which they would not have enjoyed at the time of their composition, when there may have been any number of competing poetical histories of the Trojan War.*

Exactly when these poems were lost is not known. The non-Homeric epics were universally considered to be inferior to the *Iliad* and *Odyssey*, and thus may have been less widely circulated, although they remained extant almost a thousand years after their composition. Athenaeus of Naucratis read them in the

---

* Jonathan S. Burgess, *The Tradition of the Trojan War in Homer & the Epic Cycle* (Johns Hopkins University Press, 2003)

3rd century AD, and it is probable that Quintus Smyr-naeus was at the very least familiar with the *Aethiopis, Little Iliad* and *Iliou Persis* when he composed his *Posthomerica* a century later. It is likely that copies survived in the Greek-speaking Eastern Roman Empire well into the early medieval period, but they seem to have disappeared by the 1st millennium. Photius I (c. 810 to 893 AD), Ecumenical Patriarch of Constantino-ple and Eastern Orthodox saint—who presumably had access to the entire Imperial Library of Constantinople when compiling his *Myriobiblos* ("many books")— knew them only from references in other works.

Fortunately, the literary record of the Trojan War does not begin and end with the Epic Cycle, and it remained a popular topic for poets, writers, tragedians, artists and mythographers throughout antiquity. Some years ago I set myself the task of reading all (or as much as I could then obtain) of the available material, begin-ning with the *Iliad*, then Quintus Smyrnaeus' *Postho-merica*, Sophocles' *Ajax* and *Philoctetes*, Aeschylus' *Oresteia*, then the *Odyssey*, and finishing with Virgil's *Aeneid*. In the midst of this mammoth undertaking it occurred to me that it would—theoretically—be possi-ble to reconstruct the lost Cyclic epics from later writ-ings, fusing Archaic and Classical Greek, Latin, and Byzantine texts into a veritable "Frankenstein's Mon-ster" of a document, arranged and edited in such a manner as to approximate the lost originals. A kind of literary back-breeding, carefully selecting passages for their desirable traits, and combining them to emulate an extinct progenitor. The *Cypria* seemed an appropriate starting point.

My goal was to assemble a coherent, easy-to-follow narrative with the bare minimum of editorial intervention, in as great a detail as possible while relying only on Classical sources; that is, works composed while the stories told in the *Cypria* were still a part of the public consciousness. The result—limited as it is by the fragmentary nature of the source material—may only superficially resemble the original epic, but will at least allow a reader to enjoy this lost story as a single, (mostly) uninterrupted text for the first time in over a thousand years.

With its primary function being a narrative one, this volume may be of limited interest to the seasoned Classical scholar, who will already be familiar with much—if not all—of the material presented here. Some in academia may indeed balk at the thought of these excerpts removed from their proper context and reduced to mere building blocks! This said, there is surely some value in having all of the "pre-*Iliad*" documents gathered together in one convenient volume, if only to provide the necessary back-story for anyone preparing to embark on a study of the Homeric epics.

The *Cypria* was an epic poem in eleven books, variously attributed to Homer, Hegesias of Salamis, Cyprias of Halicarnassus, or most commonly, Stasinus of Cyprus. The latter two at least provide some explanation for the title, which otherwise bears no relation to the poem's content.* According to the Byzantine poet John Tzetzes, writing in the 12th century, Stasinus was the son-in-law of Homer, gifted the *Cypria* as a dowry at his wedding. This story probably arose as a convenient means of giving the epic an Homeric pedigree, whilst at the same time acknowledging it as a lesser

---

* It has also been theorised that "Cypria" refers to "Cypris", or Aphrodite, who seems to have been prominent throughout.

work (similarly, Arctinus of Miletus, reputed author of the *Aethiopis* and *Iliou Persis*, was said to have been Homer's pupil).

The *Cypria* essentially recounted the early history of the Trojan War, from its origins at the wedding of Peleus and Thetis to the capture of Chryseis and Briseis, leading into the events of the *Iliad*. It was criticised by Aristotle for covering too much ground; its broad scope and frenetic pace resulting in a work resembling a chronicle rather than a unified story.[*] The eleven books spanned two decades; compare with the twenty-four books of the *Iliad*, which takes place over a matter of weeks.

Many of the myths originally found within the *Cypria* will be familiar to modern readers; the contest between the goddesses, Paris' abduction of Helen, and the sacrifice of Agamemnon's daughter Iphigenia. Others have all but disappeared from common knowledge. Palamedes, who rivalled Odysseus in cunning, Telephus the son of Heracles, and Protesilaus, the first man to die at Troy, were as celebrated in antiquity as Achilles and Hector, but are virtually unknown today. Perhaps it is time these forgotten heroes were given their due.

A Note on the Sources

THE great tragedy of Greek and Roman literature is that so little of it remains—in the case of many lost works all we have is a title. Others survive in fragments; a few lines on a degraded parchment, or as a

---

[*] Aristotle, *Poetics* 1459 a–b

quotation preserved in a later work. Many details, including entire lines from the lost Cyclic epics, are known from references in later writings, or as annotations on ancient manuscripts; scholiasts' explanatory notes, relating the documents at hand to the Cyclic tradition. Of the *Cypria* almost fifty lines survive in this way, although many are out of context, and their original place within the poem unknowable.

Our understanding of the Epic Cycle is largely dependent on a *Chrestomathy* ("literary summary") written by a certain Proclus, who has been cautiously identified as the 5th century Neoplatonist philosopher Proclus Lycaeus, or the 2nd century grammarian Eutychius Proclus, tutor to Marcus Aurelius—probably incorrectly in both cases. No complete text of the *Chrestomathy* survives, and its original scope is unknown, but a damaged excerpt describing the Trojan Cycle is preserved in a 10th century manuscript of the *Iliad* known as "Venetus A". The *Cypria* section is missing, but appears by itself in a number of other manuscripts. These excerpts would have provided readers with a "backdrop" for the *Iliad*, with the non-Homeric epics presumably lost at the time of their transcription.

The accuracy of Proclus' *Chrestomathy* is questionable, with the poems all seeming to fit together a little too snugly. We know from surviving fragments that there were in fact considerable overlaps between the Cyclic epics; the *Aethiopis* is known to have described the suicide of Telamonian Ajax, whereas Proclus places it in the *Little Iliad*. There is also evidence that both the *Little Iliad* and *Iliou Persis* covered the sack of Troy. These omissions may have been deliberate, so as not to confuse the readership; alternately, as

Burgess suggests, Proclus may be summarising an "edited" version of the Cycle, with the beginnings and endings of some of the poems lopped off wherever content was duplicated. In any case, the *Chrestomathy* provides a useful framework upon which to build this reconstruction.

The story of the Trojan War has not remained static over the centuries, with variances ranging from the subtle to the significant accumulating with every retelling. The Roman version of a myth cannot be expected to agree with an Attic tragedy of the 5th century BC, and yet, one cannot assume every variation from the Cyclic tradition to be a later corruption. Even when the poems of the Epic Cycle were composed there were very likely competing versions of the same myths, and there are numerous inconsistencies within the Cycle itself. The murder of Astyanax, for example, was said to have been committed by Neoptolemus in the *Little Iliad*, and Odysseus in the *Iliou Persis*. In reconstructing the *Cypria* I have endeavoured to select passages which agree with the summary by Proclus, but with the written record so patchy this was not always possible. Any known or suspected divergences have been indicated via endnotes, as well as any points where sources disagree. These sources are as follows.

Pindar (c. 522 to c. 443 BC) was a Greek lyric poet; that is, a composer of short, occasional (in contrast to epic) poetry, the performance of which was often accompanied with a lyre. His *Nemean Ode X* celebrated the victory of Theaius of Argos in a wrestling match at the Nemean Games circa 450 BC, and tells the story of "two mighty athletes", Castor and Pollux—an episode once found in the *Cypria*.

Euripides (c. 480 to 406 BC) was an Athenian

tragedian, and author of up to 95 plays of which 18 or 19 survive (the authorship of *Rhesus* is contested). The Trojan War was an enormously popular subject among Greek dramatists, but *Iphigenia at Aulis* is the only extant tragedy set during the events of the *Cypria*. Had the complete works of Euripides, Aeschylus and Sophocles survived, it might have been possible to reconstruct the entire Epic Cycle from their plays alone. The text is printed here in its entirety, and forms the centrepiece of this volume.

The *Bibliotheca* or "Library" of Apollodorus is an anthology of Greek myths, believed to date from the 1st or 2nd century AD. Early scholars erroneously identified the author with Apollodorus of Athens (b. 180 BC); the author of the *Bibliotheca* is sometimes known as *Pseudo*-Apollodorus in order to distinguish him from the Athenian. Frustratingly, surviving manuscripts are incomplete, breaking off before the story of the Trojan War. These later sections are known only from two manuscript summaries, epitomised by the Scottish anthropologist and mythographer Sir James George Fraser in the late 19th century. Even in its reduced form the *Bibliotheca* contains a wealth of invaluable material—not least due to Apollodorus helpfully naming many of his sources, most of which are now lost.

Publius Ovidius Naso, better known as "Ovid" (43 BC to AD 17 or 18), was a Roman poet during the reign of Augustus. The *Metamorphoses*—arguably his most famous work—is a collection of Greek and Roman myths bound by the common theme of physical transformation. It was immensely popular in the medieval period and Renaissance, and remains an important source for a number of myths not found elsewhere.

Gaius Julius Hyginus (64 BC to 17 AD), was a Latin author, roughly contemporary with Ovid. Peculiarly, the work for which he is chiefly known does not even survive in the author's own words. The *Fabulae*—a collection of fables similar in scope to Apollodorus' *Bibliotheca*—is preserved in a crudely written summary, referred to by scholar and essayist Arthur L. Keith in a review of H. J. Rose's 1934 edition as a "school-boy's exercise",* and it may well be exactly that. Nevertheless, the *Fabulae*—or its primitive reduction—stands alongside the *Bibliotheca* as a pillar of our modern understanding of Greek and Roman mythology.

Parthenius of Nicaea (d. 14 AD) was a Greek poet and grammarian, and a tutor of the poet Virgil. His only surviving work is the *Erotica Pathemata*—a collection of mythological and semi-historical love stories.

Colluthus was a Greek epic poet of the Byzantine city of Lycopolis (modern Asyut, Egypt), active during the reign of Anastasius I (491 to 518 AD). His only extant poem is *The Rape of Helen*, which, although its literary merit has often been called into question, does nonetheless contain the most detailed accounts of the wedding of Peleus and Thetis, the Apple of Discord, and Paris' abduction of Helen to have survived from antiquity.

Dictys Cretensis Ephemeris Belli Trojani is an interesting document, purporting to be a first-hand "Chronicle of the Trojan War" by one Dictys of Crete, a follower of King Idomeneus. It was published in Latin

* A. L. Keith, *The Classical Journal* vol. 31, no. 1 (October 1935): p.53

in the 4th century AD by a Lucius Septimius, with an epistle describing its discovery in Dictys' earthquake-damaged tomb at Cnossos during the reign of the Emperor Nero (54 to 68 AD). The text, in Phoenician letters, was reportedly inscribed on a number of wooden tablets preserved in a tin box; this was subsequently translated into Greek and presented as a gift to Nero. Three centuries later it came into the possession of Septimius, who translated it into Latin.

The work, along with the rather fanciful account of its rediscovery, was accepted as genuine by the Romans and Byzantines, but later scholars assumed it to be the invention of Septimius or an anonymous Latin author. Papyrus fragments discovered among the ruins of the Egyptian city of Tebtunis in the winter of 1899-1900 proved the existence of a Greek original, which has been supposed to date from the 1st or 2nd century AD.

In terms of its actual content the work is problematic, often being in direct conflict with other sources. Many of these contradictions are probably deliberate; that the document may assert itself as a "genuine" historical account—in contrast to the fictional retellings by the likes of Homer and his successors. The gods are largely absent, with the divine and/or supernatural elements heavily downplayed. Unfortunately, this has meant that the sections I quote from Dictys must rely on copious amounts of endnotes in order to explain these irregularities. For convenience's sake I refer to the author as "Dictys" throughout, although the actual author is unknown.

A similar document, believed to date from the 5th or early 6th century, is *Daretis Phrygii de Excidio Trojae Historia*, or "Dares of Phrygia's History of the

Fall of Troy". This is another supposedly first-hand account, written by a Trojan priest of Hephaestus a who is actually mentioned in Book V of Homer's *Iliad* when his son Phegeus is slain by Diomedes. It tells the same story from a Trojan perspective, albeit in much less detail than Dictys—the pre-*Iliad* material is very brief, and I have not quoted any passages in this volume. However, it is still worthy of mention, as it was chiefly through the lens of Dares and Dictys that medieval Europe viewed the Trojan War, with the *Iliad* and *Odyssey* inaccessible until the early modern period.

The *Excidium Troiae* or "Destruction of Troy" is ostensibly a medieval text of the late 13th century, rediscovered in 1932 by E. Bagby Atwood of the University of Texas among a quantity of manuscripts collected by Richard Rawlinson, an 18th century clergyman and antiquarian, and bequeathed to the Bodleian Library in Oxford. The work consists of a chronicle of the Trojan War from the wedding of Peleus and Thetis to the death of Achilles, an epitome of Virgil's *Aeneid*, and an account of the founding of Rome and its history up to the reign of Augustus. It was immediately clear to Atwood that the Troy portion of the *Excidium Troiae* did not derive from Dictys or Dares, which at that time were believed to be the only sources available to medieval scholars. Its version of events closely follows the original Epic Cycle, leading Atwood to conclude that it can only be derived from an unknown Roman work, possibly dating from the time of Augustus, where the chronicle ends. Thus it earns its place here as an "indirect" Classical source.

To maintain readability and consistency, in the Latin texts I have silently reverted the Roman names to their Greek forms, e.g. Ulysses becomes Odysseus;

Jupiter and Jove become Zeus. An exception has been made for names where the Latin form is more common, such as Ajax and Pollux; in such cases this rule has been applied in reverse. Similarly, Paris has been preferred to Alexander/Alexandrus, except when specifically referring to his second name.

Additionally, I have taken the liberty of changing the first person pronouns in my translation of *Dictys Cretensis Ephemeris Belli Trojani* to third person, substituting "us", "we" and "our" for "them", "they" and "their" (or simply "the Greeks"). This was deemed preferable to the narrative voice suddenly switching perspective at certain points, and does not alter the content in any meaningful way.

—D. M. Smith, 2017

CHRONOLOGY

Mycenaean Age

c. 1200 BC Proposed date of the Trojan War.

Archaic Period

c. 760-710 BC The *Iliad* and *Odyssey*.

c. 700 BC Hesiod.

c. 650-610 BC The *Cypria*.

Classical Period

480 BC Battle of Thermopylae.

c. 450 BC Pindar's *Nemean Ode X*.

431-404 BC Peloponnesian War.

405 BC Euripides' *Iphigenia at Aulis*.

Hellenistic Period

323 BC Death of Alexander the Great.

Roman Period

146 BC Roman conquest of Greece.

c. 50 BC - 14 AD   Parthenius' *Erotica Pathemata.*

c. 40 BC - 17 AD   Hyginus' *Fabulae.*

27 BC   Augustus Caesar is named *Princeps* by the Roman Senate, marking the beginning of the Roman Empire.

19 BC   Virgil's *Aeneid.*

8 AD   Ovid's *Metamorphoses.*

c. 100 AD   Apollodorus' *Bibliotheca.*

c. 120-170 AD   Pausanias' *Description of Greece.*

c. 350 AD   *Dictys Cretensis Ephemeris Belli Trojani* is published in Latin. Greek original believed to date from c. 100 AD.

c. 350-390 AD   Quintus Smyrnaeus' *Posthomerica.*

476 AD   Fall of the Western Roman Empire.

Byzantine Period

c. 500 AD   Colluthus' *The Rape of Helen.*

Medieval Period

c. 1250 AD   *Excidium Troiae.* Probably based on a lost Roman text.

1453 AD   Fall of Constantinople to the Ottoman Turks, marking the end of the Eastern Roman (Byzantine) Empire

THE CYPRIA

I.

Zeus plans with Themis[1] to bring about the Trojan war. Eris arrives while the gods are feasting at the marriage of Peleus and starts a dispute between Hera, Athena, and Aphrodite as to which of them is fairest.

The three are led by Hermes at the command of Zeus to Paris on Mount Ida for his decision, and Paris, lured by his promised marriage with Helen, decides in favour of Aphrodite.

—Proclus, *Chrestomathy*

The Plan of Zeus

THERE was a time when the countless tribes of men, though wide-dispersed, oppressed the surface of the deep-bosomed earth, and Zeus saw it and had pity and in his wise heart resolved to relieve the all-nurturing earth of men by causing the great struggle of the Ilian war, that the load of death might empty the world. And so the heroes were slain in Troy, and the plan of Zeus came to pass.[2]

—Scholiast on Homer, *Iliad*, I

1

Peleus and Thetis

TO THETIS, aged Proteus once had said, "Oh goddess of the waves, you shall conceive, and you shall be the mother of a youth who by heroic actions will surpass the deeds of his own father, and your son shall be superior to his father's power." So Zeus, although the flame of love for Thetis burned his breast, would not embrace the lovely daughter of the sea, and urged his grandson Peleus, son of Aeacus, to wed the green-haired maid without delay.[3] There is a curved bay of Haemonia, where like an arch, two bending arms project out in the waves, as if to form a harbour; but the water is not deep—although enough to hide a shoal of sand. It has a firm shore which will not retain a foot's impression, nor delay the step—no seaweeds grow in that vicinity.

There is a grove of myrtle near that place thick-hung with berries, blended of twin shades. A cave within the middle of that grove is found, and whether it was formed by art or nature is not known, although it seems a work of art. There Thetis often went, quite naked, seated on her dolphin, which was harnessed. Peleus seized her there when she was fast asleep; and after he had tried to win her by entreaties, while she long continued to resist him, he resolved to conquer her by violence, and seized her neck with both arms. She resorted then to all her usual art, and often changed her shape as it was known, so that he failed in his attempt. At first she was a bird, but while she seemed a bird he held her fast; and then she changed herself to a large tree, and Peleus clung with ardour to the tree; her third disguise was as a spotted tigress, which frightened him so that he lost his hold.

Then, as he poured wine on the heaving sea, he prayed unto the sea-green gods and gave them sacrifice of sheep entrails, and smoke of frankincense. He ceased not, till at last the prophet of Carpathia, as he rose up from a deep wave, said, "Hark unto me, oh son of Aeacus and you shall have the bride your heart desires! When she at rest lies sleeping in the cool wave, you must bind her while she is unwary, with strong cords and complicated bonds. And never let her arts deceive you when she imitates a hundred varied forms, but hold her fast, whatever she may seem, until she shall at length assume the shape she had at first." So Proteus cautioned him, and hid his face beneath the waves as his last words were said.[4]

Now Helios was descending and the pole of his bright chariot as it downward bent illuminated the Hesperian main; and at that time the lovely Nereid, Thetis, departing from her ocean wave, entered the cavern for desired repose. Peleus was waiting there. Immediately, just as he seized upon the virgin's limbs, she changed her shape and persevered until convinced she could not overcome his hold—for her two arms were forced apart—she groaned and said, "You could not overcome me in this way, but some divinity has given you the power."

Then she appeared as Thetis; and, when Peleus saw her now deprived of all deceptions, he embraced her and was father of the great Achilles.

—Ovid, *Metamorphoses*, XI

The Birth of Achilles

AND he married her on Pelion, and there the gods celebrated the marriage with feast and song. And Chiron gave Peleus an ashen spear, and Poseidon gave him horses, Balius and Xanthus, and these were immortal.[5]

When Thetis had got a babe by Peleus, she wished to make it immortal, and unknown to Peleus she used to hide it in the fire by night in order to destroy the mortal element which the child inherited from its father, but by day she anointed him with ambrosia. But Peleus watched her, and, seeing the child writhing on the fire, he cried out; and Thetis, thus prevented from accomplishing her purpose, forsook her infant son and departed to the Nereids.[6]

Peleus brought the child to Chiron, who received him and fed him on the innards of lions and wild swine and the marrows of bears, and named him Achilles, because he had not put his lips to the breast; but before that time his name was Ligyron.[7]

—Apollodorus, *Bibliotheca*, III.13.5-6

The Birth of Paris

PODARCES, who was called Priam, came to the throne, and he married first Arisbe, daughter of Merops, by whom he had a son Aesacus, who married Asterope, daughter of Cebren, and when she died he mourned for her and was turned into a bird. But Priam handed over Arisbe to Hyrtacus and married a second wife Hecuba, daughter of Dymas, or, as some say, of Cisseus, or, as others say, of the river Sangarius and Metope. The first son born to her was Hector; and when a second babe was about to be born Hecuba dreamed she had brought forth a firebrand, and that the fire spread over the whole city and burned it.

When Priam learned of the dream from Hecuba, he sent for his son Aesacus, for he was an interpreter of dreams, having been taught by his mother's father Merops. He declared that the child was begotten to be the ruin of his country and advised that the babe should be exposed. When the babe was born Priam gave it to a servant to take and expose on Ida; now the servant was named Agelaus. Exposed by him, the infant was nursed for five days by a bear; and, when he found it safe, he took it up, carried it away, brought it up as his own son on his farm, and named him Paris.

When he grew to be a young man, Paris excelled many in beauty and strength, and was afterwards surnamed Alexander, because he repelled robbers and defended the flocks.[8]

—Apollodorus, *Bibliotheca*, III.12.5

Paris Among the Herdsmen

WHEN he had grown into a young man, his foster father clothed him in the garb of a herdsman and set him to work herding the sheep and cattle, and among the herdsmen he was soon held in high esteem. Now it came to pass that a bull of uncommon size was born into Paris' herd, and when it had matured it would fight with the bulls of the other herds, and had the better of each and every one of them. And after every victory Paris would place upon its head a golden crown, between the horns.

Seeing this, the war-god Ares assumed the likeness of a bull and came down to challenge the bull of Paris. And Ares, in the shape of a bull, did contest with the bull of Paris and emerged the victor. Now Paris, seeing that Ares had defeated his champion bull, placed the crown between the war-god's horns to acknowledge his victory. Word of this contest spread, and because of his impartiality, as a judge he was said to be just.

Thus Paris was chosen by Zeus to adjudicate upon the three goddesses.

—Anonymous, *Excidium Troiae*

Paris and Oenone

WHEN Paris, Priam's son, was tending his flocks on Mount Ida, he fell in love with Oenone the daughter of [the river god] Cebren; and the story is that she was possessed by some divinity and foretold the future, and generally obtained great renown for her understanding and wisdom. Paris took her away from her father to Ida, where his pasturage was, and lived with her there as his wife, and he was so much in love with her that he would swear to her that he would never desert her, but would rather advance her to the greatest honour.

She however said that she could tell that for the moment indeed he was wholly in love with her, but that the time would come when he would cross over to Europe, and would there, by his infatuation for a foreign woman, bring the horrors of war upon his kindred. She also foretold that he must be wounded in the war, and that there would be nobody else, except herself, who would be able to cure him; but he used always to stop her, every time that she made mention of these matters. Time went on, and Paris took Helen to wife;

Oenone took his conduct exceedingly ill, and returned to Cebren.[9]

—Parthenius, *Love Romances*, IV

The Funeral Games

ONE day servants sent by Priam came to choose a bull for the forthcoming games in remembrance of Paris, and they began to lead away his favourite bull. And Paris went after them and asked them where they were taking it. They informed him that they were leading it to Priam, to be awarded to whomever should come first in the funeral games.

—Hyginus, *Fabulae*, XCI

Paris Returns to Troy

NOW a yearning came into the heart of Paris for the great event that was now taking place in Troy—a thing wholly unfamiliar to him. And he made it known to his foster father that he intended to go down to Troy, where King Priam reigned, and witness the spectacle for himself. Fearing danger, his foster father attempted to dissuade him.

"You have the spectacle of your cattle," he said. "How can you long for that which you have not seen?" But Paris' longing only increased, and seeing that he could not deter him, his foster father at last agreed to accompany him to Troy to watch the games.

When the charioteers had completed their sixth race, the wrestlers—as was the custom—came before the royal box to fight. And when Paris watched them, in the brashness of his youth he sought to join the fight. His foster father, worrying for his safety, attempted to call him back. But the impetuous youth would not be deterred, and he strode out onto the sand to join in the contest. And by sheer strength in lieu of art he overcame them all and received the crown.

The wrestlers having departed, the young runners now came forth, darting from mark to mark; into these he ran and won the crown. Then the sons of the king—even his own brothers—were moved to wrath, and came into the arena that they might compete with him. Nevertheless he defeated them, and earned his third crown.

Now the sons of the king, having been put to shame in view of all the people, began to think of how to murder him. They commanded their soldiers to station themselves at the exits of the arena, so that when the games were dismissed they could easily trap him, and thus fulfil their evil desire.

But his foster father saw what they were planning to do, and he rushed down into the arena and loudly interrupted the king. "Have mercy, your Royal Highness," he shouted, "for this child is your own! And you, sons of the king, forget this madness, for he is your brother!"

And the king did know his son, and his brothers their brother, he went to the palace and was duly recognised as their kinsman. Now when this became known to the priests they began to dread the return of Paris, recalling the dream of his mother, and they said that he ought to be slain. When this reached the ear of the king, he said: "Better the city should perish than the death of our child."

—Anonymous, *Excidium Troiae*

The Judgement of Paris

SO AMONG the high-peaked hills of the Haemonians, the marriage song of Peleus was being sung while, at the bidding of Zeus, Ganymede poured the wine. And all the race of the gods hasted to do honour to the white-armed bride, own sister of Amphitrite: Zeus from Olympus and Poseidon from the sea. Out of the land of Melisseus, from fragrant Helicon, Apollo came leading the clear-voiced choir of the Muses. On either side, fluttering with golden locks, the unshorn cluster of his hair was buffeted by the west wind. And after him followed Hera, sister of Zeus; nor did the queen of harmony herself, even Aphrodite, loiter in coming to the groves of the Centaur. Came also Peitho,[10] having fashioned a bridal wreath, carrying the quiver of archer Eros. And Athena put off her mighty helmet from her brow and followed to the marriage, albeit of marriage she was untaught. Nor did Leto's daughter Artemis, sister of Apollo, disdain to come, goddess of the wilds thought she was. And iron Ares, even as, helmetless nor lifting warlike spear, he comes into the house of Hephaestus, in such wise without breastplate and without whetted sword danced smilingly. But Eris did Chiron leave unhonoured: Chiron did not regard her, and Peleus heeded her not.

And as some heifer wanders from the pasture in the glen and roams in the lonely brush, smitten by the bloody gadfly, the goad of kine: so Eris, overcome by the pangs of angry jealousy, wandered in search of a way to disturb the banquet of the gods. And often would she leap up from her chair, set with precious stones, and anon sit down again. She smote with her hand the bosom of the earth and heeded not the rock.

Fain would she unbar the bolts of the darksome hollows and rouse the Titans from the nether pit and destroy the heaven, the seat of Zeus, who rules on high. Fain would she brandish the roaring thunderbolt of fire, yet gave way, for all her age, to Hephaestus, keeper of quenchless fire and of iron. And she thought to rouse the heavy-clashing din of shields, if haply they might leap up in terror at the noise. But from her later crafty counsel, too, she withdrew in fear of iron Ares, the shielded warrior.

And now she bethought her of the golden apples of the Hesperides. Thence Eris took the fruit that should be the harbinger of war, even the apple, and devised the scheme of signal woes. Whirling her arm she hurled into the banquet the primal seed of turmoil and disturbed the choir of goddesses. Hera, glorying to be the spouse and to share the bed of Zeus, rose up amazed, and would fain have seized it. And Aphrodite, as being more excellent than all, desired to have the apple, for that it is the treasure of the Loves.[11] But Hera would not give it up and Athena would not yield. And Zeus, seeing the quarrel of the goddesses, and calling his son Hermes, who sat below his throne, addressed him thus: "If haply, my son, thou hast heard of a son of Priam, one Paris, the splendid youth, who tends his herds on the hills of Troy, give to him the apple; and bid him judge the goddesses' meeting brows and orbèd eyes. And let her that is preferred have the famous fruit to carry away as the prize of the fairer and ornament of the Loves."

So the father, the son of Cronus, commanded Hermes. And he hearkened to the bidding of his father and led the goddesses upon the way and failed not to heed. And every goddess sought to make her beauty more desirable and fair. Aphrodite of crafty counsels unfolded her snood and undid the fragrant clasp of her hair and wreathed with gold her locks, with gold her flowing tresses. And she saw her children the Loves and called to them.

"The contest is at hand, dear children! Embrace your mother that nursed you. Today it is beauty of face that judges me. I fear to whom this herdsman will award the apple. Hera they call the holy nurse of the Graces, and they say that she wields sovereignty and holds the sceptre. And Athena they ever call the queen of battles. I only, Aphrodite, am an unwarlike goddess. I have no queenship of the gods, wield no warlike spear, nor draw the bow. But wherefore am I sore afraid, when for spear I have, as it were, a swift lance, the honeyed girdle of the Loves! I have my girdle, I ply my goad,[12] I raise my bow: even that girdle, whence women catch the sting of my desire, and travail oftentimes, but not unto death."

So spake Aphrodite of the rosy fingers and followed. And the wandering Loves heard the dear bidding of their mother and hasted after their nurse.[13]

Now they had just passed over the summit of the hill of Ida, where under a rock-crowned cliff's height young Paris herded his father's flocks. On either side the streams of the mountain torrent he tended his herds, numbering apart the herd of thronging bulls, apart measuring the droves of feeding flocks. And behind him hung floating the hide of a mountain goat, that reached right to his thighs. But his herdsman's crook, driver of kine, was laid aside; for so, walking mincingly in his accustomed ways, he pursued the shrill minstrelsy of his pipe's rustic reeds. Often as he sang in his shepherd's shieling he would forget his bulls and heed no more his sheep. Hence with his pipe, in the fair haunts of shepherds, he was making dear music to Pan and Hermes. The dogs bayed not, and the bull did not bellow. Only windy Echo with her untutored cry, answered his voice from Ida's hills; and the bulls upon the green grass, when they had eaten their fill, lay down and rested on their heavy flanks.

So as he made shrill music under the high-roofed canopy of trees, he beheld from afar the messenger Hermes. And in fear he leapt up and sought to shun the eye of the gods. He leaned against an oak his choir of musical reeds and checked his lay that had not yet laboured much. And to him in his fear wondrous Hermes spake thus: "Fling away thy milking-pail and leave thy fair flocks and come hither and give decision as judge of the goddesses of heaven. Come hither and decide which is the more excellent beauty of face, and to the fairer give this apple's lovely fruit."

So he cried. And Paris bent a gentle eye and quietly essayed to judge the beauty of each. He looked at the light of their grey eyes, he looked on the neck arrayed with gold, he marked the bravery of each; the shape of the heel behind, yea and the soles of their feet. But, before he gave judgement, Athena took him, smiling, by the hand and spake to Paris thus: "Come hither, son of Priam! Leave the spouse of Zeus and heed not Aphrodite, queen of the bridal bower, but praise thou Athena who aids the prowess of men. They say that thou art a king and keepest the city of Troy. Come hither, and I will make thee the saviour of their city to men hard pressed: lest ever Enyo[14] of grievous wrath weigh heavily upon thee. Hearken to me and I will teach thee war and prowess."

So cried Athena of many counsels, and white-armed Hera thus took up the tale: "If thou wilt elect me and bestow on me the fruit of the fairer, I will make thee lord of all mine Asia. Scorn thou the works of battle. What has a king to do with war? A prince gives command both to the valiant and to the unwarlike. Not always are the squires of Athena foremost. Swift is the doom and death of the servants of Enyo!"

Such lordship did Hera, who hath the foremost throne, offer to bestow. But Aphrodite lifted up her deep-bosomed robe and bared her breast to the air and had no shame. And lifting with her hands the honeyed girdle of the Loves she bared all her bosom and heeded not her breasts. And smilingly she thus spake to the herdsman: "Accept me and forget wars: take my beauty and leave the sceptre and the land of Asia. I know not the works of battle. What has Aphrodite to do with shields? By beauty much more do women excel. In place of manly prowess I will give thee a lovely bride, and, instead of kingship, enter thou the bed of Helen. Lacedaemon, after Troy, shall see thee a bridegroom."

Not yet had she ceased speaking and he gave her the splendid apple, beauty's offering, the great treasure of Aphrogeneia, a plant of war, of war an evil seed. And she, holding the apple in her hand, uttered her voice and spake in mockery of Hera and manly Athena: "Yield to me, accustomed as ye be to war, yield me the victory. Beauty have I loved and beauty follows me. They say that thou, mother of Ares, didst with travail bear the holy choir of the fair-tressed Graces. But today they have all denied thee and not one hast thou found to help thee. Queen but not of shields and nurse but not of fire, Ares hath not aided thee, though Ares rages with the spear: the flames of Hephaestus have not aided thee, though he brings to birth the breath of fire. And how vain is thy vaunting, Athena, whom marriage sowed not nor mother bare, but cleaving of iron and root of iron made thee spring without bed of birth from the head of thy sire! And how, covering thy body in brazen robes, thou dost flee from love and pursuest the works of Ares, untaught of harmony and knowing not of concord. Knowest thou not that such as thou are the more unvaliant—exulting in glorious wars, with limbs at feuds, neither men nor women?"

Thus spake Aphrodite and mocked Athena. So she got the prize of beauty that should work the ruin of a city, repelling Hera and indignant Athena.

—Colluthus, *The Rape of Helen*

II.

Then Paris builds his ships at Aphrodite's suggestion, and Helenus foretells the future to him, and Aphrodite orders Aeneas to sail with him, while Cassandra prophesies as to what will happen afterwards. Paris next lands in Lacedaemon and is entertained by Castor and Pollux, and afterwards by Menelaus in Sparta, where in the course of a feast he gives gifts to Helen.

After this, Menelaus sets sail for Crete, ordering Helen to furnish the guests with all they require until they depart. Meanwhile, Aphrodite brings Helen and Paris together, and they, after their union, put very great treasures on board and sail away by night. Hera stirs up a storm against them[11] and they are carried to Sidon, where Paris takes the city. From there he sailed to Troy and celebrated his marriage with Helen.

In the meantime Castor and Pollux, while stealing the cattle of Idas and Lynceus, were caught in the act, and Castor was killed by Idas, and Lynceus and Idas by Pollux. Zeus gave them immortality every other day.

—Proclus, *Chrestomathy*

The Oath of Tyndareus

ZEUS in the form of a swan consorted with Leda, and on the same night Tyndareus cohabited with her; and she bore Pollux and Helen to Zeus, and Castor and Clytemnestra to Tyndareus.[2] But some say that Helen was a daughter of Nemesis and Zeus; for that she, flying from the arms of Zeus, changed herself into a goose, but Zeus in his turn took the likeness of a swan and so enjoyed her; and as the fruit of their loves she laid an egg,[3] and a certain shepherd found it in the groves and brought and gave it to Leda; and she put it in a chest and kept it; and when Helen was hatched in due time, Leda brought her up as her own daughter. And when she grew into a lovely woman, Theseus carried her off and brought her to Aphidnae. But when Theseus was in Hades, Pollux and Castor marched against Aphidnae, took the city, got possession of Helen, and led Aethra, the mother of Theseus, away captive.[4]

Now the kings of Greece repaired to Sparta to win the hand of Helen. The wooers were these: Odysseus son of Laertes, Diomedes son of Tydeus, Antilochus son of Nestor, Agapenor son of Ancaeus, Sthenelus son of Capaneus, Amphimachus son of Cteatus, Thalpius son of Eurytus, Meges son of Phyleus, Amphilochus son of Amphiaraus, Menestheus son of Peteos, Schedius and Epistrophus, sons of Iphitus, Polyxenus son of Agasthenes, Peneleos son of Hippalcimus; Leitus son of Alector, Ajax son of Oileus; Ascalaphus and Ialmenus, sons of Ares; Elephenor son of Chalcodon, Eumelus son of Admetus, Polypoetes son of Pirithous, Leonteus son of Coronus, Podalirius and Machaon, sons of Asclepius, Philoctetes son of Poeas, Eurypylus son of Evaemon, Protesilaus son of Iphiclus; Menelaus son of Atreus, Ajax and Teucer, sons of Telamon, Patroclus son of Menoetius.[5]

Seeing the multitude of them, Tyndareus feared that the preference of one might set the others quarrelling; but Odysseus promised that, if he would help him to win the hand of Penelope, he would suggest a way by which there would be no quarrel. And when Tyndareus promised to help him, Odysseus told him to exact an oath from all the suitors that they would defend the favoured bridegroom against any wrong that might be done him in respect of his marriage. On hearing that, Tyndareus put the suitors on their oath, and while he chose Menelaus to be the bridegroom of Helen, he solicited Icarius to bestow Penelope on Odysseus.[6]

—Apollodorus, *Bibliotheca*, III.10.7-9

The Rape of Helen

AND unhappy Paris, yearning with love and pursuing one whom he had not seen, gathered men that were skilled of handicraft, and led them to a shady wood. There the oaks from Ida of many tree trunks were cut and felled by the excellent skill of Phereclus, source of woe; who at that time, doing pleasure to his frenzied king, fashioned with the wood-cutting bronze ships for Paris. On the same day he willed and on the same made the ships: ships which Athena neither planned nor wrought.

And now he had just left the hills of Ida for the deep, and, after with many a sacrifice upon the shore he had besought the favour of Aphrodite that attended him to aid his marriage, he was sailing the Hellespont over the broad back of the sea, when to him there appeared a token of his laborious toils. The dark sea leapt aloft and girdled the heaven with a chain of dusky coils and straightway poured forth rain from the murky air, and the sea was turmoiled as the oarsmen rowed.

Then when he had passed Dardania and the land

of Troy and, coasting along, left behind the mouth of the Ismarian lake, speedily, after the mountains of Thracian Pangaeon, he saw rising into view the tomb of Phyllis that loved her husband and the nine-circled course of her wandering path, where thou didst range and cry, Phyllis, waiting the safe return of thy husband Demophon, when he should come back from the land of Athena.[7]

Then across the rich land of the Haemonians there suddenly arose upon his eyes the flowery Achaean land, Phthia, feeder of men, and Mycenae of wide streets. Then past the marshes where Erymanthus rises he marked Sparta of fair women, the dear city of the son of Atreus, lying on the banks of the Eurotas. And hard by, established under a hill's shady wood, he gazed upon her neighbour, lovely Therapne. Thence they had not far to sail, nor was the noise of the oars rowing in the calm sea heard for long, when they cast the hawsers of the ship upon the shores of a fair gulf and made them fast, even they whose business was the works of the sea.

And he washed him in the snowy river and went his way, stepping with careful steps, lest his lovely feet should be defiled of the dust; lest, if he hastened more quickly, the winds should blow heavily on his helmet and stir up the locks of his hair.

And now he scanned the high-built houses of the hospitable inhabitants and the neighbouring temples hard by, and surveyed the splendour of the city; here gazing on the golden image of native Athena herself, and there passing the dear treasure of Carneian Apollo, even the shrine of Hyacinthus of Amyclae, whom once while he played as a boy with Apollo the people of Amyclae marked and marvelled whether he too had not been conceived and borne by Leto to Zeus. But Apollo knew not that he was keeping the youth for envious Zephyrus. And the earth, doing a pleasure to the weeping king, brought forth a flower to console Apollo, even that flower which bears the name of the splendid youth.[8]

And at last by the halls of the son of Atreus, builded near, he stood, glorying in his marvellous graces. Not so fair was the lovely son whom Thyone bare to Zeus: forgive me, Dionysus! Even if thou art of the seed of Zeus, he, too, was fair as his face was beautiful. And Helen unbarred the bolts of her hospitable bower and suddenly went to the court of the house, and, looking in front of the goodly doors, soon as she saw, so soon she called him and led him within the house, and bade him sit on a new-wrought chair of silver.[9]

And she could not satisfy her eyes with gazing, now deeming that she looked on the golden youth that attends on Aphrodite, and late she recognized that it was not Eros—she saw no quiver of arrows. And often in the beauty of his face and eyes she looked to see the king of the vine, but no blooming fruit of the vine did she behold spread upon the meeting of his gracious brows. And after long time, amazed, she uttered her voice and said:

"Stranger, whence art thou? Declare thy fair lineage even unto us. In beauty thou art like unto a glorious king, but thy family I know not among the Argives. I know all the family of blameless Deucalion. Not in sandy Pylos, the land of Neleus, hast thou thy dwelling: Antilochus I know, but thy face I have not seen. Not in gracious Phthia, nurse of chieftains; I know the whole renowned race of the sons of Aeacus, the beauty of Peleus, the fair fame of Telamon, the gentleness of Patroclus and the prowess of Achilles."

So, yearning for Paris, spake the lady of sweet voice. And he opened honeyed speech and answered her: "If haply thou hast heard of a town in the bounds of Phrygia—even Ilium, whereof Poseidon built the towers and Apollo—if thou hast haply heard of a very wealthy king in Troy, sprung from the fruitful race of Cronus: thence am I a prince and pursue all the works of my race. I, lady, am the dear son of Priam rich in gold, of the lineage of Dardanus am I, and Dardanus was the son of Zeus. And the gods from Olympus, companioning with men, oft-times became his servants, albeit they were immortal: of whom Poseidon with Apollo built the shining walls of our fatherland. And I, oh Queen, am the judge of goddesses. For, deciding a suit for the aggrieved daughters of heaven, I praised the beauty of Aphrodite and her lovely form. And she vowed that she would give me a worthy recompense of my labour; even a glorious and a lovely bride, whom they call Helen, sister of Aphrodite, and it is for her sake that I have endured to cross such seas. Come, let us join wedlock, since Aphrodite bids. Despise me not, put not my love to shame. I will not say—why should I tell thee who knowest so much? For thou knowest that Menelaus is of an unvaliant race. Not such as thou are women born among the Argives, for they wax with meaner limbs and have the look of men and are but bastard women."

So he spake. And the lady fixed her lovely eyes upon the ground, and long-time perplexed replied not. But at last amazed she uttered her voice and said: "Of a surety, oh stranger, did Poseidon and Apollo in days of old build the foundation of thy fatherland? Fain would I have seen those cunning works of the immortals and the shrill-blowing pasture of shepherd Apollo, where by the god-built vestibules of the gates Apollo often-times followed the kine of shuffling gait. Come now, carry me from Sparta unto Troy. I will follow, as Aphrodite, queen of wedlock, bids. I do not fear Menelaus, when Troy shall have known me."

So the fair-ankled lady plighted her troth. And night, respite from labour after the journey of the sun, lightened sleep and brought the beginning of wandering morn, and opened the two gates of dreams: one the gate of truth—it shone with the sheen of horn—whence leap forth the unerring messages of the gods; the other the gate of deceit, nurse of empty dreams. And he carried Helen from the bowers of hospitable Menelaus to the benches of his sea-faring ships, and exulting exceedingly in the promise of Aphrodite he hastened to carry to Ilium his freight of war.

And Hermione cast to the winds her veil and, as morning rose, wailed with many tears. And often taking her handmaidens outside her chamber, with shrillest cries she uttered her voice and said: "Girls, whither hath my mother gone and left me in grievous sorrow, she that yester-even with me took the keys of the chamber and entered one bed with me and fell asleep?"

So spake she weeping and the girls wailed with her. And the women gathered by the vestibule on either side and sought to stay Hermione in her lamentation: "Sorrowing child, stay thy lamentation; thy mother has gone, yet shall she come back again. While still thou weepest, thou shalt see her. Seest not? Thine eyes are blinded with tears and thy blooming cheeks are marred with much weeping. Haply she hath gone to a meeting of women in assembly and, wandering from the straight path, stands distressed; or she hath gone to the meadow and sits on the dewy plain of the Hours; or she hath gone to wash her body in the river of her fathers and lingered by the streams of Eurotas."

Then spake the sorrowful maiden weeping: "She knows the hill, she hath skill of the rivers' flow, she knows the paths to the roses, to the meadow. What say ye to me, women? The stars sleep and she rests among the rocks; the stars rise, and she comes not home. My mother, where art thou? In what hills dost thou dwell? Have wild beasts slain thee in thy wandering? But even the wild beasts tremble before the offspring of high Zeus.

"Hast thou fallen from thy car on the levels of the dusty ground, and left thy body in the lonely thickets? But I have scanned the trees of the many-trunked copses in the shady wood, yea, even to the very leaves, yet thy form have I not seen; and the wood I do not blame. Have the smooth waters covered thee in the depths, swimming in the wet streams of murmuring Eurotas? But even in the rivers and in the depths of the sea the Naiads live and do not slay women."

Thus she wailed, and leaning back her neck breathed Sleep who walks with Death; for verily it was ordained that both should have all things in common and pursue the works of the elder brother: hence women, weighed down with sorrowing eyes, oft-times, while they weep, fall asleep. And wandering amid the deceits of dreams she fancied that she saw her mother; and, amazed, the maiden, in her grief cried out: "Yesterday to my sorrow thou didst fly from me out of the house and left me sleeping on my father's bed. What mountain have I left alone? What hill have I neglected? Followest thou thus the love of fair-tressed Aphrodite?"

Then the daughter of Tyndareus spake to her and

said: "My sorrowful child, blame me not, who have suffered terrible things. The deceitful man who came yesterday hath carried me away!"

So she spake, And the maiden leapt up, and seeing not her mother, uttered a yet more piercing cry and wailed: "Birds, winged children of the brood of air, go ye to Crete, and say to Menelaus: 'Yesterday a lawless man came to Sparta and hath laid waste all the glory of thy halls!'" So spake she with many tears to the air, and seeking for her mother wandered in vain.[10]

—Colluthus, *The Rape of Helen*

Helen in Egypt

BUT some say that Hermes, in obedience to the will of Zeus, stole Helen and carried her to Egypt, and gave her to Proteus, King of the Egyptians, to guard, and that Paris repaired to Troy with a phantom of Helen fashioned out of clouds.[11]

—Apollodorus, *Bibliotheca*, E.3.5

The Sack of Sidon

PARIS departed Lacedaemon in reckless haste, and a strong wind blew him to Cyprus, forcing him to anchor there. After procuring a number of ships he sailed on to Phoenicia, and was received warmly by the king of the Sidonians. But in the night Paris set an ambush for the king, and taking him by surprise he slew him and ransacked his house, exhibiting once again that same treachery that had possessed him in Sparta. In this way every article of royal wealth was carried off to the ships.

But those who had fled the sack of the palace now raised a revolt, lamenting the death of their king. Taking up arms they marched on the palace, but by this time Paris had already carried off everything he wanted, and was now hastening to return to his homeland. The mob pursued him even to the ships, and there battle was done. Many fell on both sides; the Sidonians fighting to avenge their dead king, and the Trojans fiercely defending the wealth they had seized. During the struggle two of the Trojan ships were set aflame, but the rest managed to break free. The Sidonians meanwhile, their strength utterly spent, could do naught but watch helplessly as their enemy escaped.

—Dictys Cretensis, *Ephemeris Belli Trojani*, I

Paris and Helen Enter Troy

AND to the towns of the Cicones and the straits of Aeolian Helle, into the havens of Dardania the bridegroom brought his bride. And Cassandra on the acropolis, when she beheld the new-comer, tore her hair amain and flung away her golden veil. But Troy unbarred the bolts of her high-built gates and received on his return her citizen that was the source of her woe.

—Colluthus, *The Rape of Helen*

The Dioscuri

OF THE sons born to Leda Castor practised the art of war, and Pollux the art of boxing; and on account of their manliness they were both called Dioscuri.[12] And wishing to marry the daughters of Leucippus, they carried them off from Messene and wedded them; and Pollux had Mnesileus by Phoebe, and Castor had Anogon by Hilaira. And having driven booty of cattle from Arcadia, in company with Idas and Lynceus, sons of Aphareus, they allowed Idas to divide the spoil. He cut a cow in four and said that one half of the booty should be his who ate his share first, and that the rest should be his who ate his share second. And before they knew where they were, Idas had swallowed his own share first and likewise his brother's, and with him had driven off the captured cattle to Messene.

But the Dioscuri marched against Messene, and drove away that cattle and much else besides. And they lay in wait for Idas and Lynceus.

—Apollodorus, *Bibliotheca*, III.11.2

The Death of Castor

GAZING keenly after them from Taygetus, Lynceus beheld them sitting in ambush in the trunk of an oak. For his, of all earthly men, was the most piercing eye.[13] With nimble feet forthwith [Lynceus and Idas] arrived and quickly wrought a bold deed; the death of Castor. And grievous retribution the sons of Aphareus suffered at the hands of Zeus; for immediately the son of Leda came in hot pursuit, and they over against him took their post hard by their fathers' tomb. Thence snatching a decoration of Death, a polished [tomb]stone, they hurled it at the breast of Pollux; but they crushed him not, nor drove him back; but rushing on straightway with spear swift in motion, he drove the brass into the sides of Lynceus. And Zeus hurled upon Idas his smouldering thunderbolt, and they both were burnt together bereft of mourners; for a contest with powerful ones is hard for men to deal with.[14]

Speedily to his mighty brother the son of Tyndareus returned back, and him he found not as yet dead, but with short-drawn gasp rucking forth his breath. Then shedding warm tears with groans he cried loud and clear:

"Oh Father, son of Cronus, what end shall there be of my sorrows! For me also together with him ordain death, oh monarch. Honour is departed from the man that is deprived of his friends; and in distress few are there of mortals faithful enough to go shares in toil." Thus he spoke, and Zeus before him came and uttered this reply:

"Thou art my son; but him engendered after thee of mortal seed did her hero husband in approach to thy mother beget.[15] But come, of these things in sooth I yet give thee choice: if on the one hand thou art willing to escape death and hateful old age, and to inhabit Olympus in company with Athena and with Ares of the spear black with blood, there is to thee indeed a rightful share of this; but if in thy brother's behalf thou contendest, and art minded to share out to him an equal lot of all thou hast, then half thy life thou must breathe beneath the earth, and half in the golden abodes of heaven."

Thus then when he spoke, no wavering resolution did Pollux adopt in his mind. And Zeus unclosed the eyes and let loose the voice of the brazen-belted Castor.

—Pindar, *Nemean Ode X*

The Kingdom of Messenia

AFTER the fight about the cattle between the sons of Aphareus and their cousins the Dioscuri, when Lynceus was killed by Pollux and Idas met his doom from the lightning, the house of Aphareus was bereft of all male descendants, and the kingdom of Messenia passed to Nestor the son of Neleus, including all the part ruled formerly by Idas.

—Pausanias, *Description of Greece*, 4.3.1

III.

Iris next informs Menelaus of what has happened at his home. Menelaus returns and plans an expedition against Ilium with his brother, and then goes on to Nestor. Nestor in a digression tells him how Epopeus was utterly destroyed after seducing the daughter of Lycus, and the story of Oedipus, the madness of Heracles, and the story of Theseus and Ariadne.

—Proclus, *Chrestomathy*

Menelaus in Crete

ALL those kings who were the great-grandchildren of Minos, the son of Zeus, gathered in Crete to divide the wealth of Atreus. In his last will, Atreus the son of Minos[1] had left all of his gold, his silver, and his cattle to his grandsons; the sons of his daughters. All was to be apportioned equally, with the exception of his realm and its cities: these he bequeathed to Idomeneus and Meriones. Idomeneus was the son of Deucalion, and Meriones the son of Molus; unto them he commanded the rule of his kingdom.[2]

With them came the sons of Clymene and Nauplius, Palamedes and Oeax.[3] Also Menelaus and his elder brother Agamemnon, begotten of Aerope and Pleisthenes (by them they also had a sister, Anaxibia, who was then the wife of Nestor)[4] came to accept their share. Many believed them to be the sons of Atreus, for

28

when Pleisthenes died young and in obscurity, his deeds being held in small account, Atreus took pity on the youths and raised them as his own.[5] And when all was divided, each man received a magnificent inheritance.

Agamemnon and Menelaus received a warm welcome, with the many scions of Europa, who was worshipped as a goddess on the island,[6] coming to escort them to the temple. Many days of celebration followed, with sacrifices to the gods as befitting the customs of that land, and lavish banquets. The kings of Greece delighted in this entertainment, but still more impressive was the temple itself; so magnificent and beautiful a structure. Admiring all of its embellishments, they recalled how Phoenix, father of Europa, had carried these riches across from Sidon.

At the same time Phrygian Paris, the son of Priam, along with Aeneas[7] and a number of other relatives, was welcomed into the home of Menelaus of Sparta. There, seeing that the king was absent, he perpetrated a monstrous crime. Overcome by lust for Helen, the most beautiful woman in all of Greece, he made off with her, also taking many riches, as well as Aethra and Clymene; Menelaus' relatives who attended on Helen.

A messenger came to Crete bearing news of the crime Paris had committed in the halls of Menelaus, but also—as often occurs in such situations—rumours spread throughout the island that wildly exaggerated what had occurred. Some even said that the very kingdom had been destroyed by war.

Upon being informed of this news, Menelaus was deeply disturbed by the actions of his wife, but even more so at having been betrayed by his aforementioned relatives.[8] Palamedes, seeing the king stupefied by wrath and indignation, ordered that the ships be prepared to sail. He briefly consoled the king, as seemed fitting, and after having the ships loaded with as much of Menelaus' inheritance as the time permitted, they set sail. Blessed with a fair wind, in only a few days they returned to Sparta, where Agamemnon, Nestor, and all of those rulers who were the descendants of Pelops, having heard the news, were already assembled.

—Dictys Cretensis, *Ephemeris Belli Trojani*, I

In the account given above, Menelaus finds Nestor awaiting him at Sparta. According to Proclus, the *Cypria* had Menelaus travel to Pylos, where Nestor, in one of his famous digressions, related the following cautionary tales of love and jealousy. Here Apollodorus shall speak for the son of Neleus:

Epopeus and Oedipus

ANTIOPE was a daughter of Nycteus,[9] and Zeus had intercourse with her. When she was with child, and her father threatened her, she ran away to Epopeus at Sicyon and was married to him. In a fit of despondency Nycteus killed himself, after charging [his brother] Lycus to punish Epopeus and Antiope. Lycus marched against Sicyon, subdued it, slew Epopeus, and led Antiope away captive. On the way she gave birth to two sons at Eleurethae in Boeotia. The infants were exposed, but a neatherd[10] found and reared them, and he called the one Zethus and the other Amphion.

Now Zethus paid attention to cattle-breeding, but Amphion practised minstrelsy, for Hermes had given him a lyre. But Lycus and his wife Dirce imprisoned

Antiope and treated her despitefully. Howbeit, one day her bonds were loosed of themselves, and unknown to her keepers she came to her sons cottage, begging that they would take her in. They recognized their mother and slew Lycus, but Dirce they tied to a bull, and flung her dead body into the spring that is called Dirce after her. And having succeeded to the sovereignty they fortified the city, the stones following Amphion's lyre; and they expelled Laius. He resided in Peloponnese, being hospitably received by Pelops; and while he taught Chrysippus, the son of Pelops, to drive a chariot, he conceived a passion for the lad and carried him off.

After Amphion's death Laius succeeded to the kingdom. And he married a daughter of Menoeceus; some say that she was Jocasta, and some that she was Epicasta. The oracle had warned him not to beget a son, for the son that should be begotten would kill his father; nevertheless, flushed with wine, he had intercourse with his wife. And when the babe was born he pierced the child's ankles with brooches and gave it to a herdsman to expose. But the herdsman exposed it on Cithaeron; and the neatherds of Polybus, king of Corinth, found the infant and brought it to his wife Periboea. She adopted him and passed him off as her own, and after she had healed his ankles she called him Oedipus, giving him that name on account of his swollen feet.[11]

When the boy grew up and excelled his fellows in strength, they spitefully twitted him with being supposititious. He inquired of Periboea, but could learn nothing; so he went to Delphi and inquired about his true parents. The god told him not to go to his native land, because he would murder his father and lie with his mother. On hearing that, and believing himself to be the son of his nominal parents, he left Corinth, and riding in a chariot through Phocis he fell in with Laius driving in a chariot in a certain narrow road. And when Polyphontes, the herald of Laius, ordered him to make way and killed one of his horses because he disobeyed and delayed, Oedipus in a rage killed both Polyphontes and Laius, and arrived in Thebes.

Laius was buried by Damasistratus, king of Plataea, and Creon, son of Menoeceus, succeeded to the kingdom. In his reign a heavy calamity befell Thebes. For Hera sent the Sphinx, whose mother was Echidna and her father Typhon; and she had the face of a woman, the breast and feet and tail of a lion, and the wings of a bird. And having learned a riddle from the Muses, she sat on Mount Phicium, and propounded it to the Thebans. And the riddle was this: What is that which has one voice and yet becomes four-footed and two-footed and three-footed? Now the Thebans were in possession of an oracle which declared that they should be rid of the Sphinx whenever they had read her riddle; so they often met and discussed the answer, and when they could not find it the Sphinx used to snatch away one of them and gobble him up.

When many had perished, and last of all Creon's son Haemon, Creon made proclamation that to him who should read the riddle he would give both the kingdom and the wife of Laius. On hearing that, Oedipus found the solution, declaring that the riddle of the Sphinx referred to man; for as a babe he is four-footed, going on four limbs, as an adult he is two-footed, and as an old man he gets besides a third support in a staff. So the Sphinx threw herself from the citadel, and Oedipus both succeeded to the kingdom and unwittingly married his mother, and begat sons by her, Polynices and Eteocles, and daughters, Ismene and Antigone. But some say the children were born to him by Eurygania, daughter of Hyperphas.

When the secret afterwards came to light, Jocasta hanged herself in a noose, and Oedipus was driven from Thebes, after he had put out his eyes and cursed his sons, who saw him cast out of the city without lifting a hand to help him. And having come with Antigone to Colonus in Attica, where is the precinct of the Eumenides, he sat down there as a suppliant, was kindly received by Theseus, and died not long afterwards.

—Apollodorus, *Bibliotheca*, III.5.5-9

The Madness of Heracles

ERGINUS marched against Thebes, and after slaughtering not a few of the Thebans he concluded a treaty with them, confirmed by oaths, that they should send him tribute for twenty years, a hundred kine every year. Falling in with the heralds on their way to Thebes to demand this tribute, Heracles outraged them; for he cut off their ears and noses and hands, and having fastened them by ropes from their necks, he told them to carry that tribute to Erginus and the Minyans. Indignant at this outrage, Erginus marched against Thebes. But Heracles, having received weapons from Athena and taken the command, killed Erginus, put the Minyans to flight, and compelled them to pay double the tribute to the Thebans. And Heracles received from Creon his eldest daughter Megara as a prize of valour, and by her he had three sons, Therimachus, Creontiades, and Deicoon.

Now it came to pass that after the battle with the

Minyans Heracles was driven mad through the jealousy of Hera and flung his own children, whom he had by Megara, and two children of [his brother] Iphicles into the fire; wherefore he condemned himself to exile, and was purified by Thespius, and repairing to Delphi he inquired of the god where he should dwell.

The Pythian priestess then first called him Heracles, for hitherto he was called Alcides. And she told him to dwell in Tiryns, serving Eurystheus for twelve years and to perform the ten labours imposed on him, and so, she said, when the tasks were accomplished, he would be immortal.[12]

—Apollodorus, *Bibliotheca*, II.4.11-12

Theseus and Ariadne

WHEN [Theseus] came to Crete, Ariadne, daughter of Minos, being amorously disposed to him, offered to help him if he would agree to carry her away to Athens and have her to wife. Theseus having agreed on oath to do so, she besought Daedalus to disclose the way out of the labyrinth.

And at his suggestion she gave Theseus a clue when he went in; Theseus fastened it to the door, and, drawing it after him, entered in.[13] And having found the Minotaur in the last part of the labyrinth, he killed him by smiting him with his fists; and drawing the clue after him made his way out again. And by night he arrived with Ariadne and the children at Naxos. There Dionysus fell in love with Ariadne and carried her off; and having brought her to Lemnos he enjoyed her, and begat Thoas, Staphylus, Oenopion, and Peparethus.

In his grief on account of Ariadne, Theseus forgot

to spread white sails on his ship when he stood for port; and [his father] Aegeus, seeing from the acropolis the ship with a black sail, supposed that Theseus had perished; so he cast himself down and died.

—Apollodorus, *Bibliotheca*, E.1.8-10

IV.

Then they travel over Hellas and gather the leaders, detecting Odysseus when he pretends to be mad, not wishing to join the expedition, by seizing his son Telemachus for punishment at the suggestion of Palamedes.

—Proclus, *Chrestomathy*

The Mustering of the Greeks

WHEN Menelaus was aware of the rape, he came to Agamemnon at Mycenae, and begged him to muster an army against Troy and to raise levies in Greece. And he, sending a herald to each of the kings, reminded them of the oaths which they had sworn, and warned them to look to the safety each of his own wife, saying that the affront had been offered equally to the whole of Greece. And while many were eager to join in the expedition, some repaired also to Odysseus in Ithaca.

—Apollodorus, *Bibliotheca*, E.3.6

The Madness of Odysseus

THEY came to the island of Ithaca to recruit Odysseus, son of Laertes. It had been foretold to Odysseus that if he went to Troy he would only return home after twenty years, alone and destitute. And so, when he heard that the emissaries were coming, he feigned insanity; he put on a felt cap and joined a horse and an ox to the plough.[1] However Palamedes, when he saw this, suspected that it was a ruse. Snatching Odysseus' son Telemachus from his cradle, he laid the infant in the path of the plough and said, "Drop this pretence and come join our alliance!" Then Odysseus gave his word that he would come, and from that day on he was hostile towards Palamedes.

—Hyginus, *Fabulae*, XCV

Cinyras

MENELAUS went with Odysseus and Talthybius to Cinyras in Cyprus and tried to persuade him to join the allies. He made a present of breastplates to the absent Agamemnon, and swore he would send fifty ships, but he sent only one, commanded by the son of Mygdalion, and the rest he moulded out of earth and launched them in the sea.[2]

—Apollodorus, *Bibliotheca*, E.3.9

Achilles on Skyros

WHEN Achilles was nine years old, Calchas declared that Troy could not be taken without him; so Thetis, foreseeing that it was fated he should perish if he went to the war, disguised him in female garb and entrusted him as a maiden to Lycomedes [King of Skyros]. Bred at his court, Achilles had an intrigue with Deidamia, daughter of Lycomedes, and a son Pyrrhus[3] was born to him, who was afterwards called Neoptolemus. But the secret of Achilles was betrayed, and Odysseus, seeking him at the court of Lycomedes, discovered him by the blast of a trumpet. And in that way Achilles went to Troy.[4]

He was accompanied by Phoenix, son of Amyntor. This Phoenix had been blinded by his father on the strength of a false accusation of seduction preferred against him by his father's concubine Phthia. But Peleus brought him to Chiron, who restored his sight, and thereupon Peleus made him king of the Dolopians.

Achilles was also accompanied by Patroclus, son of Menoetius[5] and Sthenele, daughter of Acastus; or the mother of Patroclus was Periopis, daughter of Pheres, or, as Philocrates says, she was Polymele, daughter of Peleus. At Opus, in a quarrel over a game of dice, Patroclus killed the boy Clitonymus, son of Amphidamas, and flying with his father he dwelt at the house of Peleus and became a minion of Achilles.

—Apollodorus, *Bibliotheca*, III.13.8

The Greeks Assemble at Argos

ARGOS, the kingdom of Diomedes, was chosen as a good place to convene and lay plans for the coming war. Thus when the moment was right came Ajax the son of Telamon, famed for his courage as much as his physical strength, and with him Teucer, his brother. Idomeneus and Meriones, who were inseparable, arrived soon after. Following them came Nestor with Antilochus and Thrasymedes, his sons by Anaxibia. Then Peneleus came with Clonius and Arcesilaus, his cousins, then Prothoenor and Leitus, the leaders of the Boeotians. Schdius and Epistrophus arrived from Phocis, Ascalaphus and Ialmenus from Orchomenus, as well as Diores and Meges, the sons of Phyleus. Thoas too, the son of Andraemon, and Eurypylus, the son of Euaemon, from Ormenion, and then Leonteus.

Then came Achilles, the son of Peleus and Thetis; he was in the first years of his manhood, tall and handsome. Such was his zeal for the glory of war that he had already distinguished himself as a mighty champion. Even so, it must be admitted that he possessed a certain heedlessness; a savage impatience. He was accompanied by his dear friend Patroclus, and Phoenix, his guardian and teacher.

Then there were Tlepolemus the son of Heracles, and after him Phidippus and Antiphus, the grandsons of Heracles, clad in beautiful armour. After them came Protesilaus the son of Iphiclus with his brother Podarces. There too was Eumelus of Pherae, whose father Admetus had once delayed his own death by having his wife die in his stead, and Podalirius and Machaon from Tricca, the sons of Asclepius, enlisted in this campaign because of their skill in medicine. Then Philoctetes the son of Poeas, the former companion of Heracles, who had received his bow and arrows after his ascension to godhood, and handsome Nireus.

Menestheus came from Athens, and Ajax the son of Oileus from Locris. From Argos, Amiphilochus and Sthenelus; Amphilochus was the son of Amphiaraus, and the other was the son of Capaneus. With them came Euryalus, the son of Mecisteus. From Aetolia came Thersander, the son of Polynices, and last of all Demophoon and Acamas. These were all the descendants of Pelops. And there were many others hailing from various regions, some the companions of kings and others being rulers themselves, whose names it does not seem necessary to list.

When all had assembled at Argos, Diomedes supplied them with lodgings and provisions. Agamemnon distributed a great amount of gold brought from Mycenae to each individual, and thus increased their yearning for war. Then by common consent the leaders swore an oath, binding them in fellowship. Calchas, Thestor's son, who was gifted in the art of divination, ordered a hog to be brought which he divided into two parts. He aligned them east and west, and when this was done he ordered them all to draw their swords and pass between them. And then, smearing their blades with its blood, and completing the other necessary rites, they pledged themselves to war against Priam and the destruction of the entire kingdom of Troy. This done, they sacrificed many victims to Ares and Harmonia[6] in a bid to win their favour.

Then in the temple of Argive Hera they made ready to elect a leader. And so every man received a tablet, upon which he inscribed—in Phoenician letters—his choice for the commander-in-chief. In this way Agamemnon was appointed. Thus with the consent of the majority he assumed command of the undertaking, which seemed proper, as it was for the sake of his brother that they now went to war, and also because he held great wealth and power that far surpassed the other kings of Greece. Then, the command of the ships was given to Achilles, Ajax, and Phoenix. Meanwhile Palamedes, Diomedes, and Odysseus were tasked with overseeing the armies at camp; logistics and the setting of watches. Having done these things, every man returned to his own kingdom to outfit his armies for the campaign.

During this time all of Greece was inflamed with zeal for the war: armour, weapons, horses, galleys; all these things were stockpiled over the course of the next two years. And in these preparations all the young men strove to outdo one another in the performing of his military duties. But the building of ships was held to be of chief importance, lest the innumerable hosts coming from far and wide be delayed from sailing. And they were filled with great amounts of grain and other necessities; this was done upon the command of Agamemnon, so that their endeavour would not be hampered by a scarcity of provisions.

As well as ships there were many horses and chariots of war, but the greater part of the army was made up of infantry; a want of fodder in Greece made the use of cavalry prohibitive. In addition there were many people recruited who were skilled in the use of nautical equipment.

At the same time Lycian Sarpedon could not be induced to join the expedition against the Trojans; neither by the friendly persuasion of Phalidis, King of the Sidonians,[7] or with outright bribery. Indeed, already Priam had offered greater gifts, which he later doubled as a reward for Sarpedon's loyalty.

The fleet, which came together from all the different kingdoms of Greece, took all of five years to be assembled and furnished for war. And when they were ready to embark, with nothing to delay them but the absence of soldiers, the chiefs gave the signal to converge on Aulis.

—Dictys Cretensis, *Ephemeris Belli Trojani*, I

V.

All the leaders then meet together at Aulis and sacrifice. The incident of the serpent and the sparrows takes place before them, and Calchas foretells what is going to befall. After this, they put out to sea, and reach Teuthrania and sack it, taking it for Ilium. Telephus comes out to the rescue and kills Thersander the son of Polynices, and is himself wounded by Achilles. As they put out from Mysia a storm comes on them and scatters them, and Achilles first puts in at Skyros and married Deidamia, the daughter of Lycomedes, and then heals Telephus, who had been led by an oracle to go to Argos, so that he might be their guide on the voyage to Ilium.
—Proclus, *Chrestomathy*

The Catalogue of Ships

THE armament mustered in Aulis. The men who went to the Trojan war were as follows. Of the Boeotians, ten leaders: they brought forty ships. Of the Orchomenians, four: they brought thirty ships. Of the Phocians, four leaders: they brought forty ships. Of the Locrians, Ajax, son of Oeleus: he brought forty ships. Of the Euboeans, Elephenor, son of Chalcodon and Alcyone: he brought forty ships. Of the Athenians, Menestheus: he brought fifty ships. Of the Salaminians, Telamonian Ajax: he brought twelve ships.

Of the Argives, Diomedes, son of Tydeus, and his company: they brought eighty ships. Of the Mycenaeans, Agamemnon, son of Atreus and Aerope: a hundred ships. Of the Lacedaemonians, Menelaus, son of Atreus and Aerope: sixty ships. Of the Pylians, Nestor, son of Neleus and Chloris: forty ships. Of the Arcadians, Agapenor: seven ships. Of the Eleans, Amphimachus and his company: forty ships. Of the Dulichians, Meges, son of Phyleus: forty ships. Of the Cephallenians, Odysseus, son of Laertes and Anticlia: twelve ships. Of the Aetolians, Thoas, son of Andraemon and Gorge: he brought forty ships. Of the Cretans, Idomeneus, son of Deucalion: forty ships. Of the Rhodians, Tlepolemus, son of Heracles and Astyoche: nine ships. Of the Symaeans, Nireus, son of Charopus: three ships. Of the Coans, Phidippus and Antiphus, the sons of Thessalus: thirty ships.

Of the Myrmidons, Achilles, son of Peleus and Thetis: fifty ships. From Phylace, Protesilaus, son of Iphiclus: forty ships. Of the Pheraeans, Eumelus, son of Admetus: eleven ships. Of the Olizonians, Philoctetes, son of Poeas: seven ships. Of the Aeanianians, Guneus, son of Ocytus: twenty-two ships. Of the Triccaeans, Podalirius: thirty ships. Of the Ormenians, Eurypylus: forty ships. Of the Gyrtonians, Polypoetes, son of Pirithous: thirty ships. Of the Magnesians, Prothous, son of Tenthredon: forty ships.

The total of ships was one thousand and thirteen; of leaders, forty-three; of leaderships, thirty.[1]

So Agamemnon in person was in command of the whole army, and Achilles was admiral, being fifteen years old.[2]

—Apollodorus, *Bibliotheca*, E.3.11-16

The Serpent and the Sparrows

VENGEANCE would not long have been delayed, but the fierce winds raged over seas impassable, and held the ships at fishy Aulis. They could not be moved from the Boeotian land. Here, when a sacrifice had been prepared to Zeus, according to the custom of their land, and when the ancient altar glowed with fire, the Greeks observed an azure coloured snake crawling up in a plane tree near the place where they had just begun their sacrifice. Among the highest branches was a nest, with twice four birds—and those the serpent seized together with the mother-bird as she was fluttering round her loss. And every bird the serpent buried in his greedy maw.

All stood amazed: but Calchas, who perceived the truth, exclaimed, "Rejoice Pelasgian men, for we shall conquer. Troy will fall; although the toil of war must long continue—so the nine birds equal nine long years of war." And while he prophesied, the serpent, coiled about the tree, was transformed to a stone, curled crooked as a snake.

—Ovid, *Metamorphoses*, XII

The Wounding of Telephus

AFTER this the winds drove the entire Greek navy to the region of Mysia, and with the signal promptly given they steered their ships to shore. But as they attempted to land they were met by armed guards, for Telephus, the ruler of Mysia, had charged these men with protecting the region from a seaborne incursion. Accordingly, they now prohibited the Greeks from coming ashore, or even setting foot on land until their arrival had been reported to the king. But some of the men ignored their warnings and began to disembark, and as they did so the guards obstructed them with the utmost force. Seeing this, the Greek commanders would not let such violence go unanswered, and taking up arms they leapt from their ships and cut down the guards in wrath; nor did they spare those who fled in terror, slaying any within their reach.[3]

The first of those to evade the Greeks now came to warn Telephus that many thousands of hostile soldiers had landed, and having slain his watchmen now occupied the beaches; each man's fear causing him to invent some new detail. Telephus, upon hearing these reports, gathered the men he had about him and all of those who could be mustered in haste, and swiftly came to meet the Greeks. Thus the two opposing armies formed battle lines, and rushed together with great force. The men fought hand-to-hand, cutting each other to pieces, with the deaths of those around them urging them to greater violence.

There on the front line Thersander, the son of Polynices, encountered Telephus and was slain by him, but not before he had felled many enemies—among them a companion of Telephus, whom he had chosen as one of his generals for his strength and intellect. By degrees these victories had caused Thersander to become overconfident, and on account of this he was killed. His bloody body was carried from the field hoisted upon the shoulders of Diomedes, because of the fellowship that had begun with their fathers. It was then cremated, and the ashes buried in the traditional manner.[4]

But Achilles and Telamonian Ajax took notice of

the great losses they were suffering in this encounter, and divided the army into two parts. They now took the time to exhort and encourage the men, which seemed to imbue them with a fresh energy, and thus they returned to the fray with greater strength. These two generals led the onslaught, rushing into a veritable wall of enemies. In this way, being the first or among the first into every battle, they had won fame and glory amongst friend and foe alike.

Meanwhile Teuthranius, begotten of Teuthras and Auge, and thus half-brother of Telephus on his mother's side, saw Ajax winning great glory fighting against his people, and in hastening to challenge him became yet another victim of his spear. Seeing this Telephus was greatly shaken, and wishing to avenge his brother's death he attacked the enemy battle line. Having put to flight those who had stood against him, he was pursuing Odysseus through a vineyard which was located near the battlefield when he tripped on the root of a vine, and fell. It was then that Achilles, observing from afar, hurled his spear and struck the king in his left thigh. But Telephus quickly got up and extracted the weapon from his body, and protected by a band of his men who had rushed to his aid he avoided a swift death.

And now the better part of the day was spent, with both armies having fought without rest, their leaders engaged in a vigorous struggle. In fact many of the Greeks, already weary from sailing, were considerably disheartened by the presence of Telephus. He was the son of Heracles indeed; tall in stature, and endowed as he was with a strength comparable to that of his divine father. Thus with the advent of night all were glad for a respite from the battle. The Mysians returned to their homes, and the Greeks to their ships. Many men on both sides had been slain, but a greater part had suffered injury; very few had left the battlefield unscathed.

On the following days envoys were sent from both sides, so that funeral rites could be performed for those who had fallen in battle. A truce was duly arranged, and the bodies of the dead were collected, then cremated and buried.

In the meantime Tlepolemus and the brothers Antiphus and Phidippus, who were the sons of Thessalus and grandsons of Heracles, having learned that Telephus was the ruler of these parts, placed confidence in their kinship, and so they came to him and told him who they were and with whom they had sailed. After a heated discussion they accused him of aiding his enemies and betraying his own kin, for Menelaus and Agamemnon, who had assembled this great army, were the descendants of Pelops.[5] Then they told him of the crime Paris had committed in the home of Menelaus, and the rape of Helen. It was fitting, they said, on account of his kinship with the Greeks, and in particular Paris' violation of the laws of hospitality, that he should wish to aid them; even as Heracles had in his many labours, the monuments to which existed throughout the whole of Greece.

Telephus, despite the terrible agony of his wound, courteously answered that it was they who were at fault; he did not know that those who had landed upon the shores of his kingdom were his allies and kinsmen, and had he been made aware of this he would have come forth to greet them as friends. They might have enjoyed his hospitality, he said, and he would have furnished them with gifts when it was time for them to depart. But the offer to join the war against Priam he must refuse, for Astyoche, a daughter of Priam, was his wife and the mother of his son Eurypylus.[6] Then he swiftly announced to his men that they should stand down and permit the Greeks to come ashore. Tlepolemus and those who had come with him were placed under the protection of Eurypylus, and escorted back to the ships to give Agamemnon and the rest of the kings news of the peace and concord with Telephus.

Upon hearing this, the Greeks at once stopped their preparations for war. The council then sent Achilles and Ajax to meet with Telephus, and seeing that he was wracked by great pain they consoled him, and encouraged him to take heart. But Telephus, when his pain had lessened somewhat, accused the Greeks of having come without sending a messenger ahead. Then he wished to know how many among them were the descendants of Pelops, and requested that they come to meet him. So they promised to inform the others of the king's desire.

Now all of the descendants of Pelops besides Agamemnon and Menelaus gathered together and came to Telephus as one, and there was much gaiety and rejoicing when they were presented to the king. He received them as guests, and endowed them with many generous gifts.[7] Not forgetting the rest of the soldiers who waited among the ships, the munificent king also had a quantity of grain and other necessary supplies delivered to the fleet. However, observing that Agamemnon and his brother were absent, the king implored Odysseus to go forth and summon them. These therefore, having received his message, came to Telephus and exchanged gifts, as per the royal custom, then sent for Podalirius and Machaon, the sons of Asclepius, to come and heal his injury; thus they promptly came to inspect the wound and provide suitable medicine.

But when violent winds had delayed the Greeks from sailing for several days, and the conditions at sea were beginning to worsen, they approached Telephus and asked him when would be a safe time to set sail. And they learned from him that the best time to sail for Troy was at the beginning of spring, and thus the decision was made to return to Boeotia. From there, after beaching their ships, the armies went home to winter in their own kingdoms.

It was around this time that word of the Greek expedition came to Troy, the message carried by Scythian barbarians who traded back and forth across the Hellespont. Fear and anxiety seized the Trojans; many had been displeased with Paris' crime from the very beginning, deeming it an evil act against Greece, and it took little imagination to see that in the coming destruction the entire community would be held liable. Amidst all this, great care was taken by Paris and his evil advisers to enlist the aid of the neighbouring countries, and those envoys he sent were commanded to conclude their business and return as soon as possible. And so the sons of Priam hastily readied their armies, so that they might launch a pre-emptive assault and thus take the war to the Greeks.

While this was going on at Troy, Diomedes, having been informed of their plans, travelled with great speed throughout the whole of Greece warning all of the leaders of the Trojans' designs. He instructed them to stow all of the necessary implements of war and set sail as soon as possible. Not long after, everyone convened at Argos. And when all were present no one disregarded his military duty, especially Telamonian Ajax, Achilles and Diomedes, who displayed great concern and enthusiasm for the undertaking; even commissioning a fleet of new ships in preparation for the initial invasion. Thus in only a few days a fleet of fifty additional ships were completed and furnished. Eight years had elapsed since the beginning of this venture, and the ninth had now begun.

As soon as everything was ready, with the seas being calm and nothing to hinder sailing, some Scythians—who by lucky chance had landed at Argos to trade—were employed by the leaders to serve as guides. At the same time Telephus was still pained by the wound that he had received in battle against the Greeks. It had now afflicted him for some time, and having found no remedy or cure he had consulted the oracle of Apollo.

—Dictys Cretensis, *Ephemeris Belli Trojani*, II

The Healing of Telephus

TELEPHUS, because his wound was unhealed and Apollo had told him that he would be cured when the one who wounded him should turn physician, came from Mysia to Argos, clad in rags, and begged the help of Achilles, promising to show the course to steer for Troy. So Achilles healed him by scraping off the rust of his Pelion spear.[8] Accordingly, on being healed, Telephus showed the course to steer, and the accuracy of his information was confirmed by Calchas by means of his own art of divination.

—Apollodorus, *Bibliotheca*, E.3.20

VI.

When the expedition had mustered a second time at Aulis, Agamemnon, while at the chase, shot a stag and boasted that he surpassed even Artemis. At this the goddess was so angry that she sent stormy winds and prevented them from sailing. Calchas then told them of the anger of the goddess and bade them sacrifice Iphigenia to Artemis. This they attempt to do, sending to fetch Iphigenia as though for marriage with Achilles. Artemis, however, snatched her away and transported her to the Tauri, making her immortal, and putting a stag in place of the girl upon the altar.

—Proclus, *Chrestomathy*

Euripides' *Iphigenia at Aulis*

Translated by E. Coleridge

DRAMATIS PERSONAE

AGAMEMNON
ATTENDANT, *an old man*
CHORUS OF WOMEN OF CHALCIS
MENELAUS
CLYTEMNESTRA
IPHIGENIA
ACHILLES
MESSENGER

The sea-coast at Aulis. Enter AGAMEMNON *and*
ATTENDANT

AGAMEMNON Old man, come hither and stand before
my dwelling.

ATTENDANT I come; what new schemes now, King
Agamemnon?

AGAMEMNON Thou shalt hear.

ATTENDANT I am all eagerness. 'Tis little enough sleep
old age allows me and keenly it watches over my
eyes.

AGAMEMNON What can that star be, steering his course
yonder?

ATTENDANT Sirius, still shooting over the zenith on his
way near the Pleiads' sevenfold track.

AGAMEMNON The birds are still at any rate and the sea
is calm; hushed are the winds, and silence broods
over this narrow firth.

ATTENDANT Then why art thou outside thy tent; why
so restless, my lord Agamemnon? All is yet quiet
here in Aulis; the watch on the walls is not yet astir.
Let us go in.

AGAMEMNON I envy thee, old man. Aye, and every man
who leads a life secure, unknown and unrenowned;
but little I envy those in office.

ATTENDANT And yet 'tis there we place the be-all and end-all of existence.

AGAMEMNON Aye, but that is where the danger comes; and ambition, sweet though it seems, brings sorrow with its near approach. At one time the unsatisfied claims of Heaven upset our life, at another the numerous peevish fancies of our subjects shatter it.

ATTENDANT I like not these sentiments in one who is a chief. It was not to enjoy all blessings that Atreus begot thee, oh Agamemnon; but thou must needs experience joy and sorrow alike, mortal as thou art. Even though thou like it not, this is what the gods decree. But thou, after letting thy taper spread its light abroad, writest the letter which is still in thy hands and then erasest the same words again, sealing and re-opening the scroll, then flinging the tablet to the ground with floods of tears and leaving nothing undone in thy aimless behaviour to stamp thee mad. What is it troubles thee? What news is there affecting thee, my liege? Come, share with me thy story. To a loyal and trusty heart wilt thou be telling it, for Tyndareus sent me that day to form part of thy wife's dowry and to wait upon the bride with loyalty.

AGAMEMNON Leda, the daughter of Thestius, had three children, maidens: Phoebe, Clytemnestra my wife, and Helen. This last it was who had for wooers the foremost of the favoured sons of Hellas, but terrible threats of spilling his rival's blood were uttered by each of them, should he fail to win the maid. Now the matter filled Tyndareus, her father, with perplexity. At length this thought occurred to him: the suitors should swear unto each other and join right hands thereon and pour libations with burnt sacrifice, binding themselves by this curse: "Whoever wins the child of Tyndareus for wife, him will we assist, in case a rival takes her from his house and goes his way, robbing her husband of his rights; and we will march against that man in armed array and raze his city to the ground, Hellene no less than barbarian."[1]

Now when they had once pledged their word and old Tyndareus with no small cleverness had beguiled them by his shrewd device, he allowed his daughter to choose from among her suitors the one towards whom the breath of love might fondly waft her. Her choice fell on Menelaus; would she had never taken him! Anon there came to Lacedaemon from Phrygia's folk the man who, legend says, adjudged the goddesses' dispute—in robes of gorgeous hue, ablaze with gold, in true barbaric pomp—and he, finding Menelaus gone from home, carried Helen off with him to his steading on Ida, a willing paramour. Goaded to frenzy Menelaus flew through Hellas, invoking the ancient oath exacted by Tyndareus and declaring the duty of helping the injured husband. Whereat the chivalry of Hellas, brandishing their spears and donning their harness, came hither to the narrow straits of Aulis with armaments of ships and troops, with many a steed and many a car, and they chose me to captain them all for the sake of Menelaus, since I was his brother. Would that some other had gained that distinction instead of me!

But after the army was gathered and come together, we still remained at Aulis weather-bound; and Calchas, the seer, bade us in our perplexity sacrifice my own begotten child Iphigenia to Artemis, whose home is in this land, declaring that if we offered her, we should sail and sack the Phrygians' capital, but if we forbore, this was not for us. When I heard this, I commanded Talthybius with loud proclamation to disband the whole host, as I could never bear to slay daughter of mine. Whereupon my brother, bringing every argument to bear, persuaded me at last to face the crime; so I wrote in a folded scroll and sent to my wife, bidding her despatch our daughter to me on the pretence of wedding Achilles, it the same time magnifying his exalted rank and saying that he refused to sail with the Achaeans, unless a bride of our lineage should go to Phthia. Yes, this was the inducement I offered my wife, inventing, as I did, a sham marriage for the maiden.

Of all the Achaeans we alone know the real truth: Calchas, Odysseus, Menelaus and myself. But that which I then decided wrongly, I now rightly countermand again in this scroll, which thou, old man, hast found me opening and resealing beneath the shade of night. Up now and away with this missive to Argos, and I will tell thee by word of mouth all that is written herein, the contents of the folded scroll, for thou art loyal to my wife and house.

ATTENDANT Say on and make it plain, that what my tongue utters may accord with what thou hast written.

AGAMEMNON "Daughter of Leda, in addition to my first letter I now send thee word not to despatch thy daughter to Euboea's embosomed wing, to the waveless bay of Aulis; for after all we wilt celebrate our child's wedding at another time."

ATTENDANT And how will Achilles, cheated of his bride, curb the fury of his indignation against thee and thy wife?

AGAMEMNON Here also is a danger.

ATTENDANT Tell me what thou meanest.

AGAMEMNON It is but his name, not himself, that Achilles is lending, knowing nothing of the marriage or of my scheming, or my professed readiness to betroth my daughter to him for a husband's embrace.

ATTENDANT A dreadful venture thine, king Agamemnon! That thou, by promise of thy daughter's hand to the son of the goddess, wert for bringing the maid hither to be sacrificed for the Danai.

AGAMEMNON Woe is me! Ah woe! I am utterly distraught; bewilderment comes over me. Away hurry thy steps, yielding nothing to old age.

ATTENDANT In haste I go, my liege.

AGAMEMNON Sit not down by woodland founts; scorn the witcheries of sleep.

ATTENDANT Hush!

AGAMEMNON And when thou passest any place where roads diverge, cast thine eyes all round, taking heed that no mule-wain pass by on rolling wheels, bearing my daughter hither to the ships of the Danai, and thou see it not.

ATTENDANT It shall be so.

AGAMEMNON Start then from the bolted gates, and if thou meet the escort, start them back again, and drive at full speed to the abodes of the Cyclopes.[2]

ATTENDANT But tell me, how shall my message find credit with thy wife or child?

AGAMEMNON Preserve the seal which thou bearest on this scroll. Away! Already the dawn is growing grey, lighting the lamp of day yonder and the fire of the sun's four steeds; help me in my trouble.

Exit ATTENDANT

AGAMEMNON None of mortals is prosperous or happy to the last, for none was ever born to a painless life.

Exit AGAMEMNON. *Enter* CHORUS OF WOMEN OF CHALCIS

CHORUS To the sandy beach of sea-coast Aulis I came after a voyage through the tides of Euripus, leaving Chalcis on its narrow firth, my city which feedeth the waters of far-famed Arethusa near the sea, that I might behold the army of the Achaeans and the ships rowed by those god-like heroes. For our husbands tell us that fair-haired Menelaus and high-born Agamemnon are leading them to Troy on a thousand ships in quest of the lady Helen, whom herdsman Paris carried off from the banks of reedy Eurotas his guerdon from Aphrodite, when that queen of Cyprus entered beauty's lists with Hera and Pallas at the gushing fount.

Through the grove of Artemis, rich with sacrifice, I sped my course, the red blush mantling on my cheeks from maiden modesty, in my eagerness to see the soldiers' camp, the tents of the mail-clad Danai, and their gathered steeds. Two chieftains there I saw met together in council: one was Ajax, son of Oileus; the other Ajax, son of Telamon, crown of glory to the men of Salamis. And I saw Protesilaus and Pala-medes, sprung from the son of Poseidon,[3] sitting there amusing themselves with intricate figures at draughts; Diomedes too at his favourite sport of hurling quoits, and Meriones the war-god's son,[4] a marvel to mankind, stood at his side. Likewise I be-held the offspring of Laertes, who came from his is-land hills, and with him Nireus, handsomest of all Achaeans. Achilles next, that nimble runner, swift on his feet as the wind, whom Thetis bore and Chi-ron trained; him I saw upon the beach, racing in full armour along the shingle and straining every nerve to beat a team of four horses, as he sped round the track on foot. Eumelus the grandson of Pheres, their driver, was shouting when I saw him, goading on his goodly steeds, with their bits of chased gold-work; whereof the centre pair, that bore the yoke, had dappled coats picked out with white, while the trace-horses, on the outside, facing the turning-post in the course, were bays with spotted fetlocks. Close beside them Peleus' son leapt on his way, in all his harness, keeping abreast the rail by the axle-box.

Next I sought the countless fleet, a wonder to behold, that I might fill my girlish eyes with gazing, a sweet delight. The warlike Myrmidons from Phthia held the right wing with fifty swift cruisers, upon whose sterns, right at the ends, stood Nereid goddesses in golden-effigy, the ensign of Achilles' armament. Near these were moored the Argive ships in equal numbers, over which Mecisteus' son [Euryalus], whom Taulaus his grandsire reared, and Sthenelus, son of Capaneus, were in command. Next in order, Theseus' son was stationed at the head of sixty ships from Attica, having the goddess Pallas set in a winged car drawn by steeds with solid hoof—a lucky sight for mariners. Then I saw Boeotia's fleet of fifty sails decked with ensigns; these had Cadmus at the stern holding a golden dragon at the beaks of the vessels, and earth-born Leitus was their admiral.

Likewise there were ships from Phocis, and from Locris came the son of Oileus with an equal contingent, leaving famed Thronium's citadel; and from Mycenae, the Cyclopes' town, Atreus' son sent a hundred well-manned galleys, his brother being with him in command, as friend with friend, that Hellas might exact on her, who had fled her home to wed a foreigner. Also I saw upon Gerenian Nestor's prows twelve from Pylos the sign of his neighbour Alpheus, four-footed like a bull. Moreover there was a squadron of Aenianian sail under king and next the lords of Elis, stationed near them, whom all the people named Epeians; and Eurytus was lord of these; likewise he led the Taphian warriors with the white oar-blades, the subjects of Meges, son of Phyleus, who had left the isles of the Echinades, where sailors cannot land.

Lastly, Ajax, reared in Salamis, was joining his right wing to the left of those near whom he was posted, closing the line with his outermost ships—twelve barques obedient to the helm—as I heard and then saw the crews; no safe return shall he obtain, who bringeth his barbaric boats to grapple Ajax. There I saw the naval armament, but some things I heard at home about the gathered host, whereof I still have a recollection.

Enter MENELAUS *and* ATTENDANT

ATTENDANT (*as* MENELAUS *wrests a letter from him*) Strange daring thine, Menelaus, where thou hast no right!

MENELAUS Stand back! Thou carriest loyalty to thy master too far.

ATTENDANT The very reproach thou hast for me is to my credit.

MENELAUS Thou shalt rue it, if thou meddle in matters that concern thee not.

ATTENDANT Thou hadst no right to open a letter which I was carrying.

MENELAUS No, nor thou to be carrying sorrow to all Hellas.

ATTENDANT Argue that point with others, but surrender that letter to me.

MENELAUS I shall not let go.

ATTENDANT Nor yet will I let loose my hold.

MENELAUS Why then, this staff of mine will be dabbling thy head with blood ere long!

ATTENDANT To die in my master's cause were a noble death.

MENELAUS Let go! Thou art too wordy for a slave.

ATTENDANT (*seeing* AGAMEMNON *approaching*) Master, he is wronging me; he snatched thy letter violently from my grasp, Agamemnon, and will not heed the claims of right!

Enter AGAMEMNON

AGAMEMNON How now? What means this uproar at the gates, this indecent brawling?

MENELAUS My tale, not his, has the better right to be spoken.

AGAMEMNON Thou, Menelaus! What quarrel hast thou with this man; why art thou haling him hence?

Exit ATTENDANT

MENELAUS Look me in the face! Be that the prelude to my story.

AGAMEMNON Shall I, the son of Atreus, close my eyes from fear?

MENELAUS Seest thou this scroll, the bearer of a shameful message?

AGAMEMNON I see it, yes; and first of all surrender it.

MENELAUS No, not till I have shown its contents to all the Danai.

AGAMEMNON What! Hast thou broken the seal and dost know already what thou shouldst never have known?

MENELAUS Yes, I opened it and know to thy sorrow the secret machinations of thy heart.

AGAMEMNON Where didst thou catch my servant? Ye gods what a shameless heart thou hast!

MENELAUS I was awaiting thy daughter's arrival at the camp from Argos.

AGAMEMNON What right hast thou to watch my doings?

MENELAUS My wish to do it gave the spur, for I am no slave to thee.

AGAMEMNON Infamous! Am I not to be allowed the management of my own house?

MENELAUS No, for thou thinkest crooked thoughts; one thing now, another formerly, and something different presently.

AGAMEMNON Most exquisite refining on evil themes! A hateful thing the tongue of cleverness!

MENELAUS Aye, but a mind unstable is an unjust possession, disloyal to friends. Now I am anxious to test thee, and seek not thou from rage to turn aside from the truth, nor will I on my part overstrain the case. Thou rememberest when thou wert all eagerness to captain the Danai against Troy, making a pretence of declining, though eager for it in thy heart; how humble thou wert then! Taking each man by the hand and keeping open doors for every fellow townsman who cared to enter, affording each in turn a chance to speak with thee—even though some desired it not—seeking by these methods to purchase popularity from all bidders.

Then when thou hadst secured the command, there came a change over thy manners; thou wert no longer so cordial before to whilom friends, but hard of access, seldom to be found at home. But the man of real worth ought not to change his manners in the hour of prosperity, but should then show himself most staunch to friends, when his own good fortune can help them most effectually. This was the first cause I had to reprove thee, for it was here I first discovered thy villainy. But afterwards, when thou camest to Aulis with all the gathered hosts of Hellas, thou wert of no account; no! The want of a favourable breeze filled thee with consternation at the chance dealt out by Heaven.

Anon the Danai began demanding that thou shouldst send the fleet away instead of vainly toiling on at Aulis; what dismay and confusion was then depicted in thy looks, to think that thou, with a thousand ships at thy command, hadst not occupied the plains of Priam with thy armies! And thou wouldst ask my counsel, "What am I to do? What scheme can I devise? Where find one?" to save thyself being stripped of thy command and losing thy fair fame. Next when Calchas bade thee offer thy daughter in sacrifice to Artemis, declaring that the Danai should then sail, thou wert overjoyed, and didst gladly undertake to offer the maid, and of thine own accord—never allege compulsion!—thou art sending word to thy wife to despatch thy daughter hither on pretence of wedding Achilles. This is the same air that heard thee say it, and after all thou turnest round and hast been caught recasting thy letter to this effect, "I will no longer be my daughter's murderer." Exactly so!

Countless others have gone through this phase in their conduct of public affairs; they make an effort while in power, and then retire dishonourably, sometimes owing to the senselessness of the citizens, sometimes deservedly, because they are too feeble of themselves to maintain their watch upon the state. For my part, I am more sorry for our unhappy Hellas, whose purpose was to read these worthless foreigners a lesson, while now she will let them escape and mock her, thanks to thee and thy daughter. May I never then appoint a man to rule my country or lead its warriors because of kinship! Ability is what the general must have, since any man with ordinary intelligence can govern a state.

CHORUS For brethren to come to words and blows, whenever they disagree, is terrible.

AGAMEMNON I wish to rebuke thee in turn, briefly, not lifting mine eyes too high in shameless wise, but in more sober fashion, as a brother; for it is a good man's way to be considerate. Prithee, why this burst of fury, these bloodshot eyes? Who wrongs thee? What is it thou wantest? Thou art fain to win a virtuous bride. Well, I cannot supply thee; for she, whom thou once hadst, was ill controlled by thee. Am I then, a man who never went astray, to suffer for thy sins? Or is it my popularity that galls thee? No! It is the longing thou hast to keep a fair wife in thy embrace, casting reason and honour to the winds. A bad man's pleasures are like himself. Am I mad, if I change to wiser counsels, after previously deciding amiss? Thine is the madness rather in wishing to recover a wicked wife, once thou hadst lost her—a stroke of Heaven-sent luck.

Those foolish suitors swore that oath to Tyndareus in their longing to wed; but Hope was the goddess that led them on, I trow, and she it was that brought it about rather than thou and thy mightiness. So take the field with them! They are ready for it in the folly of their hearts; for the deity is not without insight, but is able to discern where oaths have been wrongly pledged or forcibly extorted. I will not slay my children, nor shall thy interests be prospered by justice in thy vengeance for a worthless wife, while I am left wasting, night and day, in sorrow for what I did to one of my own flesh and blood, contrary to all law and justice. There is thy answer shortly given, clear and easy to understand; and if thou wilt not come to thy senses, I shall do the best for myself.

CHORUS This differs from thy previous declaration, but there is good in it—thy child's reprieve.

MENELAUS Ah me, how sad my lot! I have no friends then after all.

AGAMEMNON Friends thou hast, if thou seek not their destruction.

MENELAUS Where wilt thou find any proof that thou art sprung from the same sire as I?

AGAMEMNON Thy moderation, not thy madness do I share by nature.

MENELAUS Friends should sympathise with friends in sorrow.

AGAMEMNON Claim my help by kindly service, not by paining me.

MENELAUS So thou hast no mind to share this trouble with Hellas?

AGAMEMNON No, Hellas is diseased like thee according to some god's design.

MENELAUS Go vaunt thee then on thy sceptre, after betraying thine own brother! While seek some different means and other friends.

Enter MESSENGER

MESSENGER Agamemnon, lord of all Hellenes! I am come and bring thee thy daughter, whom thou didst call Iphigenia in thy home; and her mother, thy wife Clytemnestra, is with her, and the child Orestes, a sight to gladden thee after thy long absence from thy palace. But, as they had been travelling long and far, they are now refreshing their tender feet at the waters of a fair spring—they and their horses, for we turned these loose in the grassy meadow to browse their fill. I am come as their forerunner to prepare thee for their reception; for the army knows already of thy daughter's arrival, so quickly did the rumour spread. All the folk are running together to the sight, that they may see thy child; for Fortune's favourites enjoy a worldwide fame and have all eyes fixed on them. "Is it a wedding?" some ask, "or what is happening? Or has King Agamemnon from fond yearning summoned his daughter hither?" From others thou wouldst have heard: "They are presenting the maiden to Artemis, queen of Aulis, previous to marriage; who can the bridegroom be, that is to lead her home?"

Come, then, begin the rites—that is the next step—by getting the baskets ready. Crown your heads;

prepare the wedding-hymn, thou and prince Mene-
laus with thee. Let flutes resound throughout the
tents with noise of dancer's feet, for this is a happy
day that is come for the maid.

AGAMEMNON Thou hast my thanks. Now go within,
for the rest it will be well, as Fate proceeds.

Exit MESSENGER

AGAMEMNON Ah, woe is me! Unhappy wretch, what
can I say? Where shall I begin? Into what cruel
straits have I been plunged! Fortune has outwitted
me, proving far cleverer than any cunning of mine.
What an advantage humble birth possesses! For it is
easy for her sons to weep and tell out all their sor-
rows, while to the high-born man come these same
sorrows, but we have dignity throned over our life
and are the people's slaves. I, for instance, am
ashamed to weep, nor less, poor wretch, to check my
tears at the awful pass to which I am brought.

Oh! What am I to tell my wife? How shall I wel-
come her? With what face meet her? For she too has
undone me by coming uninvited in this my hour of
sorrow; yet it was but natural she should come with
her daughter to prepare the bride and perform the
fondest duties, where she will discover my villainy.
And for this poor maid—why maid? Death, me-
thinks, will soon make her his bride—how I pity her!
Thus will she plead to me, I trow: "My father, will
thou slay me? Be such the wedding thou thyself
mayst find, and whosoever is a friend to thee!" while
Orestes, from his station near us, will cry in childish

accents, inarticulate, yet fraught with meaning. Alas! To what utter ruin Paris, the son of Priam, the cause of these troubles, has brought me by his union with Helen!

CHORUS I pity her myself, in such wise as a woman, and she a stranger, may bemoan the misfortunes of royalty.

MENELAUS (*offering his hand*) Thy hand, brother! Let me grasp it.

AGAMEMNON I give it; thine is the victory, mine the sorrow.

MENELAUS By Pelops our reputed grandsire and Atreus our father I swear to tell thee the truth from my heart, without any covert purpose, but only what I think. The sight of thee in tears made me pity thee, and in return I shed a tear for thee myself; I withdraw from my former proposals, ceasing to be a cause of fear to thee. Yea, and I will put myself in thy present position; and I counsel thee, slay not thy child nor prefer my interests to thine. It is not just that thou shouldst grieve, while I am glad, or that thy children should die, while mine still see the light of day. What is it, after all, I seek? If I am set on marriage, could I not find a bride as choice elsewhere? Was I to lose a brother—the last I should have lost—to win a Helen, getting bad for good?

I was mad, impetuous as a youth, till I perceived, on closer view, what slaying children really meant. Moreover I am filled with compassion for the hapless maiden, doomed to bleed that I may wed, when I reflect that we are kin. What has thy daughter to do with Helen? Let the army be disbanded and leave Aulis; dry those streaming eyes, brother, and provoke me not to tears. Whatever concern thou hast in oracles that affect thy child, let it be none of mine; into thy hands I resign my share therein. A sudden change, thou'lt say, from my fell proposals! A natural course for me; affection for my brother caused the change. These are the ways of a man not void of virtue, to pursue on each occasion what is best.

CHORUS A generous speech, worthy of Tantalus, the son of Zeus! Thou dost not shame thy ancestry.

AGAMEMNON I thank thee, Menelaus, for this unexpected suggestion; 'tis an honourable proposal, worthy of thee.

MENELAUS Sometimes love, sometimes the selfishness of their families causes a quarrel between brothers; I loathe a relationship of this kind which is bitterness to both.

AGAMEMNON 'Tis useless, for circumstances compel me to carry out the murderous sacrifice of my daughter.

MENELAUS How so? Who will compel thee to slay thine own child?

AGAMEMNON The whole Achaean army here assembled.

MENELAUS Not if thou send her back to Argos.

AGAMEMNON I might do that unnoticed, but there will be another thing I cannot.

MENELAUS What is that? Thou must not fear the mob too much.

AGAMEMNON Calchas will tell the Argive host his oracles.

MENELAUS Not if he be killed ere that—an easy matter.

AGAMEMNON The whole tribe of seers is a curse with its ambition.

MENELAUS Yes, and good for nothing and useless, when amongst us.

AGAMEMNON Has the thought, which is rising in my mind, no terrors for thee?

MENELAUS How can I understand thy meaning, unless thou declare it?

AGAMEMNON The son of Sisyphus knows all.

MENELAUS Odysseus cannot possibly hurt us.[5]

AGAMEMNON He was ever shifty by nature, siding with the mob.

MENELAUS True, he is enslaved by the love of popularity; a fearful evil.

AGAMEMNON Bethink thee then, will he not arise

among the Argives and tell them the oracles that Calchas delivered, saying of me that I undertook to offer Artemis a victim, and after all am proving false? Then, when he has carried the army away with him, he will bid the Argives slay us and sacrifice the maiden. And if I escape to Argos, they will come and destroy the place, razing it to the ground, Cyclopean walls and all. That is my trouble. Woe is me! To what straits Heaven has brought me at this pass! Take one precaution for me, Menelaus, as thou goest through the host, that Clytemnestra learn this not, till I have taken my child and devoted her to death, that my affliction may be attended with the fewest tears. (*Turning to the* CHORUS) And you, ye stranger dames, keep silence.

Exeunt AGAMEMNON *and* MENELAUS

CHORUS Happy they who find the goddess come in moderate might, sharing with self-restraint in Aphrodite's gift of marriage and enjoying calm and rest from frenzied passions, while the Love-god, golden-haired, stretches his charmed bow with arrows twain, and one is aimed at happiness, the other at life's confusion. Oh Lady Cypris, queen of beauty![6] Far from my bridal bower I ban the last. Be mine delight in moderation and pure desires, and may I have a share in love, but shun excess therein.

Men's natures vary, and their habits differ, but true virtue is always manifest. Likewise the training that comes of education conduces greatly to virtue; for not only is modesty wisdom, but it has also the rare grace of seeing by its better judgment what is right;

whereby glory, ever young, is shed over life by repu-
tation. A great thing it is to follow virtue's foot-
steps—for women in their secret loves; while in men
again an inborn sense of order, shown in countless
ways, adds to a city's greatness.

Thou camest, oh Paris, to the place where thou wert
reared to herd the kine amid the white heifers of Ida,
piping in foreign strain and breathing on thy reeds
an echo of the Phrygian airs Olympus played.

Full-uddered cows were browsing at the spot where
that verdict 'twixt goddesses was awaiting thee the
cause of thy going to Hellas to stand before the ivory
palace, kindling love in Helen's trancéd eyes and
feeling its flutter in thine own breast; whence the
fiend of strife brought Hellas with her chivalry and
ships to the towers of Troy.

Oh, great is the bliss the great enjoy! Behold Iphige-
nia, the king's royal child, and Clytemnestra, the
daughter of Tyndareus; how proud their lineage!
How high their pinnacle of fortune! These mighty
ones, whom wealth attends, are very gods in the eyes
of less favoured folk.

Halt we here, maidens of Chalcis, and lift the queen
from her chariot to the ground without stumbling,
supporting her gently in our arms, with kind intent,
that the renowned daughter of Agamemnon but just
arrived may feel no fear. Strangers ourselves, avoid
we aught that may disturb or frighten the strangers
from Argos.

Enter CLYTEMNESTRA *and* IPHIGENIA

CLYTEMNESTRA I take this as a lucky omen, thy kindness and auspicious greeting, and have good hope that it is to a happy marriage I conduct the bride. (*To the* CHORUS) Take from the chariot the dowry I am bringing for my daughter and convey it within with careful heed.

My daughter, leave the horse-drawn car, planting thy faltering footstep delicately. (*To the* CHORUS) Maidens, take her in your arms and lift her from the chariot, and let one of you give me the support of her hand, that I may quit my seat in the carriage with fitting grace.

Some of you stand at the horses' heads, for the horse has a timid eye, easily frightened. Here, take this child Orestes, son of Agamemnon, babe as he still is.

What, sleeping, little one, tired out by thy ride in the chariot? Awake to bless thy sister's wedding; for thou, my gallant boy, shalt get by this marriage a kinsman gallant as thyself, the Nereid's godlike offspring. Come hither to thy mother, my daughter Iphigenia, and seat thyself beside me, and stationed near show my happiness to these strangers. Yes, come hither and welcome the sire thou lovest so dearly.

Hail my honoured lord, King Agamemnon! We have obeyed thy commands and are come.

Enter AGAMEMNON

IPHIGENIA (*throwing herself into* AGAMEMNON'S *arms*) Be not wroth with me, Mother, if I run from thy side and throw myself on my father's breast. Oh my father! I long to outrun others and embrace thee after this long while, for I yearn to see thy face. Be not wroth with me.

CLYTEMNESTRA Thou mayst do so, Daughter; for of all the children I have born, thou hast ever loved thy father best.

IPHIGENIA I see thee, Father, joyfully after a long season.

AGAMEMNON And I thy father thee. Thy words do equal duty for both of us.

IPHIGENIA All hail, Father! Thou didst well in bringing me hither to thee.

AGAMEMNON I know not how I am to say yes or no to that, my child.

IPHIGENIA Ha! How wildly thou art looking, spite of thy joy at seeing me.

AGAMEMNON A man has many cares when he is king and general too.

IPHIGENIA Be mine, all mine today; turn not unto moody thoughts.

AGAMEMNON Why so I am, all thine today; I have no other thought.

IPHIGENIA Then smooth thy knitted brow, unbend and smile.

AGAMEMNON Lo! My child, my joy at seeing thee is even as it is.

IPHIGENIA And hast thou then the teardrop streaming from thy eyes?

AGAMEMNON Aye, for long is the absence from each other that awaits us.

IPHIGENIA I know not, dear father mine, I know not of what thou art speaking.

AGAMEMNON Thou art moving my pity all the more by speaking so sensibly.

IPHIGENIA My words shall turn to senselessness, if that will cheer thee more.

AGAMEMNON (*aside*) Ah, woe is me! This silence is too much. (*To* IPHIGENIA) Thou hast my thanks.

IPHIGENIA Stay with thy children at home, Father.

AGAMEMNON My own wish! But to my sorrow I may not humour it.

IPHIGENIA Ruin seize their warring and the woes of Menelaus!

AGAMEMNON First will that, which has been my life-long ruin, bring ruin unto others.

IPHIGENIA How long thou wert absent in the bays of Aulis!

AGAMEMNON Aye, and there is still a hindrance to my sending the army forward.

IPHIGENIA Where do men say the Phrygians live, Father?

AGAMEMNON In a land where I would Paris, the son of Priam, never had dwelt.

IPHIGENIA 'Tis a long voyage thou art bound on, Father, after thou leavest me.

AGAMEMNON Thou wilt meet thy father again, my daughter.

IPHIGENIA Ah! Would it were seemly that thou shouldst take me as a fellow-voyager!

AGAMEMNON Thou too hast a voyage to make to a haven where thou wilt remember thy father.

IPHIGENIA Shall I sail thither with my mother or alone?

AGAMEMNON All alone, without father or mother.

IPHIGENIA What! Hast thou found me a new home, Father?

AGAMEMNON Enough of this! 'Tis not for girls to know such things.

IPHIGENIA Speed home from Troy, I pray thee, Father, as soon as thou hast triumphed there.

AGAMEMNON There is a sacrifice I have first to offer here.

IPHIGENIA Yea, 'tis thy duty to heed religion with aid of holy rites.

AGAMEMNON Thou wilt witness it, for thou wilt be standing near the laver.

IPHIGENIA Am I to lead the dance then round the altar, Father?

AGAMEMNON (*aside*) I count thee happier than myself because thou knowest nothing. (*To* IPHIGENIA) Go within into the presence of maidens, after thou hast given me thy hand and one sad kiss, on the eve of thy lengthy sojourn far from thy father's side. Bosom, cheek, and golden hair! Ah, how grievous ye have found Helen and the Phrygians' city! I can no more; the tears come welling to my eyes the moment I touch thee.

Exit IPHIGENIA

AGAMEMNON (*turning to* CLYTEMNESTRA) Herein I crave thy pardon, daughter of Leda, if I showed excessive grief at the thought of resigning my daughter to Achilles. For though we are sending her to taste of bliss, still it wrings a parent's heart when he, the father who has toiled so hard for them, commits his children to the homes of strangers.

78

CLYTEMNESTRA I am not so void of sense. Bethink thee, I shall go through this as well, when I lead the maiden from the chamber to the sound of the marriage-hymn. Wherefore I chide thee not, but custom will combine with time to make the smart grow less. As touching him to whom thou hast betrothed our daughter, I know his name, 'tis true, but would fain learn his lineage and the land of his birth.

AGAMEMNON There was one Aegina, the daughter of Asopus.

CLYTEMNESTRA Who wedded her? Some mortal or a god?

AGAMEMNON Zeus, and she bare Aeacus, the prince of Cenone.

CLYTEMNESTRA What son of Aeacus secured his father's halls?

AGAMEMNON Peleus, who wedded the daughter of Nereus.

CLYTEMNESTRA With the god's consent, or when he had taken her in spite of gods?

AGAMEMNON Zeus betrothed her, and her guardian gave consent.

CLYTEMNESTRA Where did he marry her? Amid the billows of the sea?

AGAMEMNON In Chiron's home, at sacred Pelion's foot.

CLYTEMNESTRA What! The abode ascribed to the race of Centaurs?

AGAMEMNON It was there the gods celebrated the marriage feast of Peleus.

CLYTEMNESTRA Did Thetis or his father train Achilles?

AGAMEMNON Chiron brought him up, to prevent his learning the ways of the wicked.

CLYTEMNESTRA Ah, wise the teacher, still wiser the father who entrusted his son to such hands.

AGAMEMNON Such is the future husband of thy daughter.

CLYTEMNESTRA A blameless lord; but what city in Hellas is his?

AGAMEMNON He dwells on the banks of the river Apidanus, in the borders of Phthia.

CLYTEMNESTRA Wilt thou convey our daughter thither?

AGAMEMNON He who takes her to himself will see to that.

CLYTEMNESTRA Happiness attend the pair! Which day will he marry her?

AGAMEMNON As soon as the full moon comes to give its blessing.

CLYTEMNESTRA Hast thou already offered the goddess

a sacrifice to usher in the maiden's marriage?

AGAMEMNON I am about to do so; that is the very thing
I was engaged in.

CLYTEMNESTRA Wilt thou celebrate the marriage-feast
thereafter?

AGAMEMNON Yes, when I have offered a sacrifice
required by Heaven of me.

CLYTEMNESTRA But where am I to make ready the feast
for the women?

AGAMEMNON Here beside our gallant Argive ships.

CLYTEMNESTRA Finely here! But still I must; good come
of it for all that!

AGAMEMNON I will tell thee, lady, what to do; so obey
me now.

CLYTEMNESTRA Wherein? For I was ever wont to yield
thee obedience.

AGAMEMNON Here, where the bridegroom is, will!

CLYTEMNESTRA Which of my duties will ye perform in
the mother's absence?

AGAMEMNON Give thy child away with help of Danai.

CLYTEMNESTRA And where am I to be the while?

AGAMEMNON Get thee to Argos, and take care of thy unwedded daughters.[7]

CLYTEMNESTRA And leave my child? Then who will raise her bridal torch?

AGAMEMNON I will provide the proper wedding torch.

CLYTEMNESTRA That is not the custom; but thou thinkest lightly of these things.

AGAMEMNON It is not good thou shouldst be alone among a soldier-crowd.

CLYTEMNESTRA It is good that a mother should give her own child away.

AGAMEMNON Aye, and that those maidens at home should not be left alone.

CLYTEMNESTRA They are in safe keeping, pent in their maiden-bowers.

AGAMEMNON Obey.

CLYTEMNESTRA Nay, by the goddess-queen of Argos! Go, manage matters out of doors; but in the house it is my place to decide what is proper for maidens at their wedding.

Exit CLYTEMNESTRA

AGAMEMNON Woe is me! My efforts are baffled; I am disappointed in my hope, anxious as I was to get my wife out of sight. Foiled at every point, I form my plots and subtle schemes against my best-beloved. But I will go, in spite of all, with Calchas the priest, to inquire the goddess' good pleasure—fraught with ill-luck as it is to me, and with trouble to Hellas. He who is wise should keep in his house a good and useful wife or none at all.

Exit AGAMEMNON

CHORUS They say the Hellenes' gathered host will come in arms aboard their ships to Simois with its silver eddies, even to Ilium, the plain of Troy beloved by Phoebus; where famed Cassandra, I am told, whenever the god's resistless prophecies inspire her, wildly tosses her golden tresses, wreathed with crown of verdant bay. And on the towers of Troy and round her walls shall Trojans stand, when sea-borne troops with brazen shields row in on shapely ships to the channels of the Simois, eager to take Helen, the sister of that heavenly pair whom Zeus begat, from Priam, and bear her back to Hellas by toil of Achaea's shields and spears. Encircling Pergamus, the Phrygians' town, with murderous war around her stone-built towers, dragging men's heads backward to cut their throats, and sacking the citadel of Troy from roof to base, a cause of many tears to maids and Priam's wife. And Helen, the daughter of Zeus, shall weep in bitter grief because she left her lord.

Oh! Never may there appear to me or to my children's children the prospect which the wealthy Lydian dames and Phrygia's brides will have, as at their looms they hold converse: "Say who will pluck this fair blossom from her ruined country, tightening his grasp on lovely tresses till the tears flow? 'Tis all through thee, the offspring of the long-necked swan; if indeed it be a true report that Leda bare thee to a winged bird, when Zeus transformed himself thereto, or whether, in the pages of the poets, fables have carried these tales to men's ears idly, out of season."

Enter ACHILLES

ACHILLES Where in these tents is Achaea's general? Which of his servants will announce to him that Achilles, the son of Peleus, is at his gates seeking him? For this delay at the Euripus is not the same for all of us. There be some, for instance, who, though still unwed, have left their houses desolate and are idling here upon the beach, while others are married and have children; so strange the longing for this expedition that has fallen on their hearts by Heaven's will. My own just plea must I declare, and whoso else hath any wish will speak for himself. Though I have left Pharsalia and Peleus, still I linger here by reason of these light breezes at the Euripus, restraining my Myrmidons, while they are ever instant with me saying, "Why do we tarry, Achilles? How much longer must we count the days to the start for Ilium? Do something, if thou art so minded; else lead home thy men, and wait not for the tardy action of these Atridae."

Enter CLYTEMNESTRA

CLYTEMNESTRA Hail to thee, son of the Nereid goddess! I heard thy voice from within the tent and therefore came forth.

ACHILLES Oh modesty revered! Who can this lady be whom I behold, so richly dowered with beauty's gifts?

CLYTEMNESTRA No wonder thou knowest me not, seeing I am one thou hast never before set eyes on; I praise thy reverent address to modesty.

ACHILLES Who art thou, and wherefore art thou come to the mustering of the Danai—thou, a woman, to a fenced camp of men?

CLYTEMNESTRA The daughter of Leda I; my name Clytemnestra, and my husband King Agamemnon.

ACHILLES Well and shortly answered on all important points! But it ill befits that I should stand talking to women.

CLYTEMNESTRA Stay; why seek to fly? Give me thy hand, a prelude to a happy marriage.

ACHILLES What is it thou sayest? I give thee my hand? Were I to lay a finger where I have no right, I could never meet Agamemnon's eye.

CLYTEMNESTRA The best of rights hast thou, seeing it is my child thou wilt wed, oh son of the sea-goddess whom Nereus begat.

ACHILLES What wedding dost thou speak of? Words fail

me, lady; can thy wits have gone astray and art thou inventing this?

CLYTEMNESTRA All men are naturally shy in the presence of new relations, when these remind them of their wedding.

ACHILLES Lady, I have never wooed daughter of thine, nor have the sons of Atreus ever mentioned marriage to me.

CLYTEMNESTRA What can it mean? Thy turn now to marvel at my words, for thine are passing strange to me.

ACHILLES Hazard a guess that we can both do in this matter, for it may be we are both correct in our statements.

CLYTEMNESTRA What! Have I suffered such indignity? The marriage I am courting has no reality, it seems; I am ashamed of it.

ACHILLES Someone perhaps has made a mock of thee and me. Pay no heed thereto; make light of it.

CLYTEMNESTRA Farewell; I can no longer face thee with unfaltering eyes, after being made a liar and suffering this indignity.

ACHILLES 'Tis "farewell" too I bid thee, lady; and now I go within the tent to seek thy husband.

ATTENDANT (*calling through the tent door*) Stranger of

the race of Aeacus, stay awhile! Ho there! Thee I mean, oh goddess-born, and thee, daughter of Leda.

ACHILLES Who is it calling through the half-opened door? What fear his voice betrays!

ATTENDANT A slave am I; of that I am not proud, for fortune permits it not.

ACHILLES Whose slave art thou? Not mine, for mine and Agamemnon's goods are separate.

ATTENDANT I belong to this lady who stands before the tent; a gift to her from Tyndareus her father.

ACHILLES I am waiting. Tell me, if thou art desirous, why thou hast stayed me.

ATTENDANT Are ye really all alone here at the door?

CLYTEMNESTRA To us alone wilt thou address thyself; come forth from the king's tent.

ATTENDANT (*coming out*) Oh Fortune and my own foresight, preserve whom I desire!

ACHILLES That speech will save them—in the future; it has a certain pompous air.

CLYTEMNESTRA Delay not for the sake of touching my right hand, if there is aught that thou wouldst say to me.

ATTENDANT Well, thou knowest my character and my

devotion to thee and thy children.

CLYTEMNESTRA I know thou hast grown old in the service of my house.

ATTENDANT Likewise thou knowest it was in thy dowry King Agamemnon received me.

CLYTEMNESTRA Yes, thou camest to Argos with me, and hast been mine this long time past.

ATTENDANT True; and though I bear thee all goodwill, I like not thy lord so well.

CLYTEMNESTRA Come, come, unfold whatever thou hast to say.

ATTENDANT Her father, he that begat her, is on the point of slaying thy daughter with his own hand.

CLYTEMNESTRA How? Out upon thy story, old dotard! Thou art mad.

ATTENDANT Severing with a sword the hapless maid's white throat.

CLYTEMNESTRA Ah, woe is me! Is my husband haply mad?

ATTENDANT Nay; sane, except where thou and thy daughter are concerned—there he is mad.

CLYTEMNESTRA What is his reason? What vengeful fiend impels him?

ATTENDANT Oracles—at least so Calchas says, in order that the host may start.

CLYTEMNESTRA Whither? Woe is me, and woe is thee, thy father's destined victim!

ATTENDANT To the halls of Dardanus, that Menelaus may recover Helen.

CLYTEMNESTRA So Helen's return then was fated to affect Iphigenia?

ATTENDANT Thou knowest all; her father is about to offer thy child to Artemis.

CLYTEMNESTRA But that marriage—what pretext had it for bringing me from home?

ATTENDANT An inducement to thee to bring thy daughter cheerfully, to wed her to Achilles.

CLYTEMNESTRA On a deadly errand art thou come, my daughter—both thou, and I, thy mother.

ATTENDANT Piteous the lot of both of you—and fearful Agamemnon's venture.

CLYTEMNESTRA Alas! I am undone; my eyes can no longer stem their tears.

ATTENDANT What more natural than to weep the loss of thy children?

CLYTEMNESTRA Whence, old man, dost say thou hadst this news?

ATTENDANT I had started to carry thee a letter referring to the former writing.

CLYTEMNESTRA Forbidding or combining to urge my bringing the child to her death?

ATTENDANT Nay, forbidding it, for thy lord was then in his sober senses.

CLYTEMNESTRA How comes it then, if thou wert really bringing me a letter, that thou dost not now deliver into my hands?

ATTENDANT Menelaus snatched it from me—he who caused this trouble.

CLYTEMNESTRA Dost thou hear that, son of Peleus, the Nereid's child?

ACHILLES I have been listening to the tale of thy sufferings, and I am indignant to think I was used as a tool.

CLYTEMNESTRA They will slay my child; they have tricked her with thy marriage.

ACHILLES Like thee I blame thy lord, nor do I view it with mere indifference.

CLYTEMNESTRA No longer will I let shame prevent my kneeling to thee, a mortal to one goddess-born; why do I affect reserve? Whose interests should I consult before my child's? (*Throwing herself before* ACHILLES) Oh! Help me, goddess-born, in my sore distress, and her that was called thy bride in vain, 'tis true, yet called she was. For thee it was I wreathed her head and led her forth as if to marriage, but now it is to slaughter I am bringing her. On thee will come reproach because thou didst not help her; for though not wedded to her, yet wert thou the loving husband of my hapless maid in name at any rate.

By thy beard, right hand, and mother too I do implore thee; for thy name it was that worked my ruin, and thou art bound to stand by that. Except thy knees I have no altar whereunto to fly, and not a friend stands at my side. Thou hast heard the cruel abandoned scheme of Agamemnon. I, a woman, am come as thou seest, to a camp of lawless sailor-folk, bold in evil's cause, though useful when they list; wherefore if thou boldly stretch forth thine arm in my behalf, our safety is assured. But if thou withhold it, we are lost.

CHORUS A wondrous thing is motherhood, carrying with it a potent spell, wherein all share, so that for their children's sake they will endure affliction.

ACHILLES My proud spirit is stirred to range aloft, but it has learnt to grieve in misfortune and rejoice in high prosperity with equal moderation. For these are the men who can count on ordering all their life aright by wisdom's rules. True, there are cases where 'tis pleasant not to be too wise, but there are others where some store of wisdom helps. Brought up in godly Chiron's halls myself, I learnt to keep a single heart; and provided the Atridae lead aright, I will

91

obey them. But when they cease therefrom, no more will I obey. Nay, but here and in Troy I will show the freedom of my nature, and, as far as in me lies, do honour to Ares with my spear.

Thee, lady, who hast suffered so cruelly from thy nearest and dearest, will I, by every effort in a young man's power, set right, investing thee with that amount of pity. Never shall thy daughter, after being once called my bride, die by her father's hand. For I will not lend myself to thy husband's subtle tricks; no! For it will be my name that kills thy child, although it wieldeth not the steel. Thy own husband is the actual cause, but I shall no longer be guiltless, if, because of me and my marriage, this maiden perishes; she that hath suffered past endurance and been the victim of affronts most strangely undeserved. So am I made the poorest wretch in Argos; I a thing of naught, and Menelaus counting for a man! No son of Peleus I, but the issue of a vengeful fiend, if my name shall serve thy husband for the murder.

Nay! By Nereus, who begat my mother Thetis, in his home amid the flowing waves, never shall King Agamemnon touch thy daughter, no! Not even to the laying of a fingertip upon her robe; else will Sipylus—that frontier town of barbarism, the cradle of those chieftains' line—be henceforth a city indeed, while Phthia's name will nowhere find mention. Calchas the seer shall rue beginning the sacrifice with his barley-meal and lustral water. Why, what is a seer? A man who with luck tells the truth sometimes, with frequent falsehoods, but when his luck deserts him, collapses then and there.

It is not to secure a bride that I have spoken thus—
there be maids unnumbered eager to have my love—
no! But King Agamemnon has put an insult on me;
he should have asked my leave to use my name as a
means to catch the child, for it was I chiefly who in-
duced Clytemnestra to betroth her daughter to me.
Verily I had yielded this to Hellas, if that was where
our going to Ilium broke down; I would never have
refused to further my fellow soldiers' common inter-
est. But as it is, I am as naught in the eyes of those
chieftains, and little they reck of treating me well or
ill. My sword shall soon know if anyone is to snatch
thy daughter from me, for then will I make it reek
with the bloody stains of slaughter, ere it reach
Phrygia. Calm thyself then; as a god in his might I
appeared to thee, without being so, but such will I
show myself for all that.

CHORUS Son of Peleus, thy words are alike worthy of
thee and that sea-born deity, the holy goddess.

CLYTEMNESTRA Ah! Would I could find words to utter
thy praise without excess, and yet not lose the gra-
ciousness thereof by stinting it; for when the good
are praised, they have a feeling, as it were, of hatred
for those who in their praise exceed the mean. But I
am ashamed of intruding a tale of woe, since my af-
fliction touches myself alone and thou art not affect-
ed by troubles of mine. But still it looks well for the
man of worth to assist the unfortunate, even when
he is not connected with them. Wherefore pity us,
for our sufferings cry for pity. In the first place, I
have harboured an idle hope in thinking to have thee
wed my daughter; and next, perhaps, the slaying of

my child will be to thee an evil omen in thy wooing hereafter, against which thou must guard thyself.

Thy words were good, both first and last; for if thou will it so, my daughter will be saved. Wilt have her clasp thy knees in suppliant wise? 'Tis no maid's part; yet if it seem good to thee, why come she shall with the modest look of free-born maid. But if I shall obtain the self-same end from thee without her coming, then let her abide within, for there is dignity in her reserve; still reserve must only go as far as the case allows.

ACHILLES Bring not thou thy daughter out for me to see, lady, nor let us incur the reproach of the ignorant; for an army, when gathered together without domestic duties to employ it, loves the evil gossip of malicious tongues. After all, should ye supplicate me, ye will attain a like result as if I had never been supplicated; for I am myself engaged in a mighty struggle to rid you of your troubles. One thing be sure thou hast heard; I will not tell a lie. If I do that or idly mock thee, may I die, but live if I preserve the maid.

CLYTEMNESTRA Bless thee for ever succouring the distressed!

ACHILLES Hearken then to me, that the matter may succeed.

CLYTEMNESTRA What is thy proposal? For hear thee I must.

ACHILLES Let us once more urge her father to a better frame of mind.

CLYTEMNESTRA He is something of a coward, and fears the army too much.

ACHILLES Still argument overthroweth argument.

CLYTEMNESTRA Cold hope indeed; but tell me what I must do.

ACHILLES Entreat him first not to slay his children, and if he is stubborn, come to me. For if he consents to thy request, my intervention need go no further, since this consent ensures thy safety. I too shall show myself in a better light to my friend, and the army will not blame me, if I arrange the matter by reason rather than force; while, should things turn out well, the result will prove satisfactory both to thee and thy friends, even without my interference.

CLYTEMNESTRA How sensibly thou speakest! I must act as seemeth best to thee; but should I fail of my object, where am I to see thee again? Whither must I turn my wretched steps and find thee ready to champion my distress?

ACHILLES I am keeping watch to guard thee, where occasion calls, that none see thee passing through the host of Danai with that scared look. Shame not thy father's house, for Tyndareus deserveth not to be ill spoken of, being a mighty man in Hellas.

CLYTEMNESTRA 'Tis even so. Command me; I must

play the slave to thee. If there are gods, thou for thy righteous dealing wilt find them favourable; if there are none, what need to toil?

Exeunt ACHILLES *and* CLYTEMNESTRA

CHORUS What wedding-hymn was that which raised its strains to the sound of Libyan flutes, to the music of the dancer's lyre, and the note of the pipe of reeds?

'Twas in the day Pieria's fair-tressed choir came over the slopes of Pelion to the marriage-feast of Peleus, beating the ground with print of golden sandals at the banquet of the gods, and hymning in dulcet strains the praise of Thetis and the son of Aeacus, over the Centaurs' hill, down through the woods of Pelion.

There was the Dardanian boy, Phrygian Ganymede, whom Zeus delights to honour, drawing off the wine he mixed in the depths of golden bowls; while, along the gleaming sand, the fifty daughters of Nereus graced the marriage with their dancing, circling in a mazy ring.

Came too the revel-rout of Centaurs, mounted on horses, to the feast of the gods and the mixing-bowl of Dionysus, leaning on fir-trees, with wreaths of green foliage round their heads; and loudly cried the prophet Chiron, skilled in arts inspired by Phoebus; "Daughter of Nereus, thou shalt bear a son"— whose name he gave—"a dazzling light to Thessaly; for he shall come with an army of spearmen to the far-famed land of Priam, to set it in a blaze, his body cased in a suit of golden mail forged by Hephaestus, a gift from his goddess-mother, even from Thetis who bore him."

Then shed the gods a blessing on the marriage of the high-born bride, who was first of Nereus' daughters, and on the wedding of Peleus. But thee, will Argives crown, wreathing the lovely tresses of thy hair, like a dappled mountain hind brought from some rocky cave or a heifer undefiled, and staining with blood thy human throat; though thou wert never reared like these amid the piping and whistling of herdsmen, but at thy mother's side, to be decked one day by her as the bride of a son of Inachus.[8] Where now does the face of modesty or virtue avail aught? Seeing that godlessness holds sway, and virtue is neglected by men and thrust behind them, lawlessness over law prevailing, and mortals no longer making common cause to keep the jealousy of gods from reaching them.

CLYTEMNESTRA (*reappearing from the tent*) I have come from the tent to look out for my husband, who went away and left its shelter long ago; while that poor child, my daughter, hearing of the death her father designs for her, is in tears, uttering in many keys her piteous lamentation. (*Catching sight of* AGAMEMNON) It seems I was speaking of one not far away; for there is Agamemnon, who will soon be detected in the commission of a crime against his own child.

Enter AGAMEMNON

AGAMEMNON Daughter of Leda, 'tis lucky I have found thee outside the tent, to discuss with thee in our daughter's absence subjects not suited for the ears of maidens on the eve of marriage.

CLYTEMNESTRA What, pray, is dependent on the present crisis?

AGAMEMNON Send the maiden out to join her father, for the lustral water stands there ready, and barley-meal to scatter with the hand on the cleansing flame, and heifers to be slain in honour of the goddess Artemis, to usher in the marriage, their black blood spouting from them.

CLYTEMNESTRA Though fair the words thou usest, I know not how I am to name thy deeds in terms of praise.

Come forth, my daughter; full well thou knowest what is in thy father's mind. Take the child Orestes, thy brother, and bring him with thee in the folds of thy robe.

Enter IPHIGENIA

CLYTEMNESTRA Behold! She comes, in obedience to thy summons. Myself will speak the rest alike for her and me.

AGAMEMNON My child, why weepest thou and no longer lookest cheerfully? Why art thou fixing thine eyes upon the ground and holding thy robe before them?

CLYTEMNESTRA Alas! With which of my woes shall I begin? For I may treat them all as first, or put them last or midway anywhere.

AGAMEMNON How now? I find you all alike, confusion and alarm in every eye.

CLYTEMNESTRA My husband, answer frankly the questions I ask thee.

AGAMEMNON There is no necessity to order me; I am willing to be questioned.

CLYTEMNESTRA Dost thou mean to slay thy child and mine?

AGAMEMNON (*starting*) Ha! These are heartless words, unwarranted suspicions!

CLYTEMNESTRA Peace! Answer me that question first.

AGAMEMNON Put a fair question and thou shalt have a fair answer.

CLYTEMNESTRA I have no other questions to put; give me no other answers.

AGAMEMNON Oh fate revered, oh destiny, and fortune mine!

CLYTEMNESTRA Aye, and mine and this maid's too; the three share one bad fortune.

AGAMEMNON Whom have I injured?

CLYTEMNESTRA Dost thou ask me this question? A thought like that itself amounts to thoughtlessness.

AGAMEMNON Ruined! My secret out!

CLYTEMNESTRA I know all; I have heard what thou art bent on doing to me. Thy very silence and those frequent groans are a confession; tire not thyself by telling it.

AGAMEMNON Lo! I am silent; for, if I tell thee a falsehood, needs must I add effrontery to misfortune.

CLYTEMNESTRA Well, listen, for I will now unfold my meaning and no longer employ dark riddles. In the first place—to reproach thee first with this—it was not of my own free will but by force that thou didst take and wed me, after slaying Tantalus, my former husband, and dashing my babe on the ground alive, when thou hadst torn him from my breast with brutal violence. Then, when those two sons of Zeus, who were likewise my brothers, came flashing on horseback to war with thee, Tyndareus, my aged sire, rescued thee because of thy suppliant prayers, and thou in turn hadst me to wife. Once reconciled to thee upon this footing, thou wilt bear me witness I have been a blameless wife to thee and thy family, chaste in love, an honour to thy house, that so thy coming in might be with joy and thy going out with gladness. And 'tis seldom a man secures a wife like this, though the getting of a worthless woman is no rarity.

Besides three daughters, of one of whom thou art heartlessly depriving me, I am the mother of this son of thine. If anyone asks thee thy reason for slaying her, tell me, what wilt thou say? Or must say it for thee? "It is that Menelaus may recover Helen." An honourable exchange, indeed, to pay a wicked woman's price in children's lives! 'Tis buying what we most detest with what we hold most dear. Again, if thou go forth with the host, leaving me in thy halls, and art long absent at Troy, what will my feelings be at home, dost think? When I behold each vacant chair and her chamber now deserted, and then sit down alone in tears, making ceaseless lamentation for her: "Ah! My child, he that begat thee hath slain thee himself, he and no one else, nor was it by another's hand."

And what might befall when thou shouldst return to thy home, after leaving such a price to be paid? For it needs now but a trifling pretext for me and the daughters remaining to give thee the reception it is right thou shouldst receive.[9] I adjure thee by the gods: compel me not to sin against thee, nor sin thyself. Go to; suppose thou sacrifice the child; what prayer wilt thou utter, when 'tis done? What will the blessing be that thou wilt invoke upon thyself as thou art slaying our daughter? An ill returning maybe, seeing the disgrace that speeds thy going forth. Is it right that I should pray for any luck to attend thee? Surely we should deem the gods devoid of sense, if we harboured a kindly feeling towards murderers.

Shalt thou embrace thy children on thy coming back
to Argos? Nay, thou hast no right. Will any child of
thine ever face thee, if thou have surrendered one of
them to death? Has this ever entered into thy calcu-
lations, or does thy one duty consist in carrying a
sceptre about and marching at the head of an army?
When thou might have made this fair proposal
among the Argives; "Is it your wish, Achaeans, to
sail for Phrygia's shores? Why then, cast lots whose
daughter has to die." For that would have been a
fair course for thee to pursue, instead of picking out
thy own child for the victim and presenting her to
the Danai; or Menelaus, inasmuch as it was his con-
cern, should have slain Hermione for her mother. As
it is, I, who still am true to thee, must lose my child;
while she, who went astray, will return with her
daughter and live in happiness at Sparta. If I am
wrong in aught herein, answer me; but if my words
have been fairly urged, do not still slay thy child,
who is mine too, and thou wilt be wise.

CHORUS Hearken to her Agamemnon, for to join in
saving thy children's lives is surely a noble deed—
none would gainsay this.

IPHIGENIA Had I the eloquence of Orpheus, my father,
to move the rocks by chanted spells to follow me, or
to charm by speaking whom I would, I had resorted
to it. But as it is, I'll bring my tears—the only art I
know—for that I might attempt. And about thy
knees, in suppliant wise, I twine my limbs; these
limbs thy wife here bore. Destroy me not before my
time, for sweet is to look upon the light, and force
me not to visit scenes below. I was the first to call

thee father, thou the first to call me child; the first
was I to sit upon thy knee and give and take the
fond caress. And this was what thou then wouldst
say, "Shall I see thee, my child, living a happy pros-
perous life in a husband's home one day, in a man-
ner worthy of myself?" And I in my turn would ask,
as I hung about thy beard, whereto I now am cling-
ing, "How shall I see thee? Shall I be giving thee a
glad reception in my halls, Father, in thy old age, re-
paying all thy anxious care in rearing me?"

I remember all we said; 'tis thou who hast forgotten
and now wouldst take my life. By Pelops, I entreat
thee spare me, by thy father Atreus and my mother
here, who suffers now a second time the pangs she
felt before when bearing me! What have I to do with
the marriage of Paris and Helen? Why is his coming
to prove my ruin, Father? Look upon me; one
glance, one kiss bestow, that this at least I may carry
to my death as a memorial of thee, though thou heed
not my pleading. (*Holding up the babe* ORESTES)
Feeble ally though thou art, brother, to thy loved
ones, yet add thy tears to mine and entreat our fa-
ther for thy sister's life—even in babes there is a nat-
ural sense of ill. Oh Father, see this speechless sup-
plication made to thee. Pity me; have mercy on my
tender years! Yea, by thy beard we two fond hearts
implore thy pity, the one a babe, a full-grown maid
the other. By summing all my pleas in one, I will
prevail in what I say. To gaze upon yon light is
man's most cherished gift; that life below is nothing-
ness, and whoso longs for death is mad. Better live a
life of woe than die a death of glory!

CHORUS Ah, wretched Helen! Awful the struggle that has come to the sons of Atreus and their children, thanks to thee and those marriages of thine.

AGAMEMNON While loving my own children, I yet understand what should move my pity and what should not—I were a madman else. 'Tis terrible for me to bring myself to this, nor less terrible is it to refuse, Daughter; for I must fare the same. Ye see the vastness of yon naval host, and the numbers of bronze-clad warriors from Hellas, who can neither make their way to Ilium's towers nor raze the far-famed citadel of Troy, unless I offer thee according to the word of Calchas the seer. Some mad desire possesses the host of Hellas to sail forthwith to the land of the barbarians, and put a stop to the rape of wives from Hellas, and they will slay my daughters in Argos as well as you and me if I disregard the goddess' behests. It is not Menelaus who hath enslaved me to him, child, nor have I followed wish of his; nay, 'tis Hellas, for whom I must sacrifice thee whether I will or no. To this necessity I bow my head; for her freedom must be preserved, as far as any help of thine, Daughter, or mine can go. Nor must they, who are the sons of Hellas, be pillaged of their wives by barbarian robbery.

AGAMEMNON *rushes from the stage*

CLYTEMNESTRA My child! Ye stranger ladies! Woe is me for this thy death! Thy father flies, surrendering thee to Hades.

IPHIGENIA Woe is me, oh Mother mine! For the same

104

strain hath fallen to both of us in our fortune. No more for me the light of day! No more the beams of yonder sun! Woe for that snow-beat glen in Phrygia and the hills of Ida, where Priam once exposed a tender babe, torn from his mother's arms to meet a deadly doom—even Paris, called the child of Ida in the Phrygians' town. Would Priam never had settled him, the herdsman reared amid the herds, beside that water crystal-clear, where are fountains of the Nymphs and their meadow rich with blooming flowers, where hyacinths and rosebuds blow for goddesses to gather! Hither one day came Pallas and Cypris of the subtle heart, Hera too and Hermes messenger of Zeus. Cypris, proud of the longing she causes; Pallas of her prowess; and Hera of her royal marriage with King Zeus, to decide a hateful strife about their beauty. But it is my death, maidens— fraught, 'tis true, with glory to the Danai—that Artemis has received as an offering, before they begin the voyage to Ilium.

Oh Mother, Mother! He that begat me to this life of sorrow has gone and left me all alone. Ah! Woe is me! A bitter, bitter sight for me was Helen, evil Helen! To me now doomed to bleed and die, slaughtered by an impious sire.

I would this Aulis had never received in its havens here the sterns of their bronze-beaked ships, the fleet which was speeding them to Troy. And would that Zeus had never breathed on the Euripus a wind to stop the expedition, tempering, as he doth, a different breeze to different men, so that some have joy in setting sail, and sorrow some, and others hard constraint, to make some start and others stay and others furl their sails! Full of trouble then, it seems, is the race of mortals, full of trouble verily; and 'tis ever Fate's decree that man should find distress.

Woe! Woe to thee, thou child of Tyndareus, for the suffering and anguish sore, which thou art causing the Danai!

CHORUS I pity thee for thy cruel fate—a fate I would thou never hadst met!

IPHIGENIA Oh Mother that bare me! I see a throng of men approaching.

CLYTEMNESTRA It is the goddess-born thou seest, child, for whom thou camest hither.

IPHIGENIA (*calling into the tent*) Open the tent-door to me, servants, that I may hide myself.

CLYTEMNESTRA Why seek to fly, my child?

IPHIGENIA I am ashamed to face Achilles.

CLYTEMNESTRA Wherefore?

IPHIGENIA The luckless ending to our marriage causes me to feel abashed.

CLYTEMNESTRA No time for affectation now in face of what has chanced. Stay then; reserve will do no good, if only we can—

Enter ACHILLES

ACHILLES Daughter of Leda, lady of sorrows!

CLYTEMNESTRA No misnomer that.

ACHILLES A fearful cry is heard among the Argives.

CLYTEMNESTRA What is it? Tell me.

ACHILLES It concerns thy child.

CLYTEMNESTRA An evil omen for thy words.

ACHILLES They say her sacrifice is necessary.

CLYTEMNESTRA And is there no one to say a word against them?

ACHILLES Indeed I was in some danger myself from the tumult.

CLYTEMNESTRA In danger of what, kind sir?

ACHILLES Of being stoned.

CLYTEMNESTRA Surely not for trying to save my daughter?

ACHILLES The very reason.

CLYTEMNESTRA Who would have dared to lay a finger on thee?

ACHILLES The men of Hellas, one and all.

CLYTEMNESTRA Were not thy Myrmidon warriors at

thy side?

ACHILLES They were the first who turned against me.

CLYTEMNESTRA My child! We are lost; undone, it seems.

ACHILLES They taunted me as the man whom marriage had enslaved.

CLYTEMNESTRA And what didst thou answer them?

ACHILLES I craved the life of her I meant to wed.

CLYTEMNESTRA Justly so.

ACHILLES The wife her father promised me.

CLYTEMNESTRA Aye, and sent to fetch from Argos.

ACHILLES But I was overcome by clamorous cries.

CLYTEMNESTRA Truly the mob is a dire mischief.

ACHILLES But I will help thee for all that.

CLYTEMNESTRA Wilt thou really fight them single-handed?

ACHILLES Dost see these warriors here, carrying my arms?

CLYTEMNESTRA Bless thee for thy kind intent!

ACHILLES Well, I shall be blessed.

CLYTEMNESTRA Then my child will not be slaughtered now?

ACHILLES No, not with my consent at any rate.

CLYTEMNESTRA But will any of them come to lay hands on the maid?

ACHILLES Thousands of them, with Odysseus at their head.

CLYTEMNESTRA The son of Sisyphus?

ACHILLES The very same.

CLYTEMNESTRA Acting for himself or by the army's order?

ACHILLES By their choice—and his own.

CLYTEMNESTRA An evil choice indeed, to stain his hands in blood!

ACHILLES But I will hold him back.

CLYTEMNESTRA Will he seize and bear her hence against her will?

ACHILLES Aye, by her golden hair no doubt.

CLYTEMNESTRA What must I do, when it comes to that?

ACHILLES Keep hold of thy daughter.

CLYTEMNESTRA Be sure that she shall not be slain, as far as that can help her.

ACHILLES Believe me, it will come to this.

IPHIGENIA Mother, hear me while I speak, for I see that thou art wroth with thy husband to no purpose; 'tis hard for us to persist in impossibilities. Our thanks are due to this stranger for his ready help; but thou must also see to it that he is not reproached by the army, leaving us no better off and himself involved in trouble. Listen, Mother; hear what thoughts have passed across my mind. I am resolved to die, and this I fain would do with honour, dismissing from me what is mean. Towards this now, Mother, turn thy thoughts, and with me weigh how well I speak.

To me the whole of mighty Hellas looks; on me the passage over the sea depends. On me the sack of Troy, and in my power it lies to check henceforth barbarian raids on happy Hellas—if ever in the days to come they seek to seize her daughters, when once they have atoned by death for the violation of Helen's marriage by Paris. All this deliverance will my death ensure, and my fame for setting Hellas free will be a happy one. Besides, I have no right at all to cling too fondly to my life; for thou didst not bear me for myself alone, but as a public blessing to all Hellas. What! Shall countless warriors, armed with shields, those myriads sitting at the oar, find courage to attack the foe and die for Hellas, because their fatherland is wronged, and my one life prevent all this? What kind of justice is that? Could I find a word in answer?

110

Now turn we to that other point. It is not right that this man should enter the lists with all Argos or be slain for a woman's sake. Better a single man should see the light than ten thousand women. If Artemis is minded to take this body, am I, a weak mortal, to thwart the goddess? Nay, that were impossible. To Hellas I resign it; offer this sacrifice and make an utter end of Troy. This is my enduring monument; marriage, motherhood, and fame—all these is it to me. And it is but right, Mother, that Hellenes should rule barbarians, but not barbarians Hellenes, those being slaves while these are free.

CHORUS Thou playest a noble part, maiden; but sickly are the whims of Fate and the goddess.

ACHILLES Daughter of Agamemnon, if some god was bent on blessing me, could I but have won thee for my wife. In thee I reckon Hellas happy, and thee in Hellas. For this that thou hast said is good and worthy of thy fatherland; since thou, abandoning a strife with heavenly powers, which are too strong for thee, has fairly weighed advantages and needs. But now that I have looked into thy noble nature, I feel still more a fond desire to win thee for my bride. Look to it, for I would fain serve thee and receive thee in my halls; and witness Thetis, how I grieve to think I shall not save thy life by doing battle with the Danai. Reflect, I say; a dreadful ill is death.

IPHIGENIA This I say, without regard to anyone. Enough that the daughter of Tyndareus is causing wars and bloodshed by her beauty; then be not slain thyself, sir stranger, nor seek to slay another on my account; but let me, if I can, save Hellas.

ACHILLES Heroic spirit! I can say no more to this, since thou art so minded; for thine is a noble resolve. Why should not one avow the truth? Yet will I speak, for thou wilt haply change thy mind; that thou mayst know then what my offer is, I will go and place these arms of mine near the altar, resolved not to permit thy death but to prevent it. For brave as thou art, at sight of the knife held at thy throat, thou wilt soon avail thyself of what I said. So I will not let thee perish through any thoughtlessness of thine, but will go to the temple of the goddess with these arms and await thy arrival there.

Exit ACHILLES

IPHIGENIA Mother, why so silent, thine eyes wet with tears?

CLYTEMNESTRA I have reason, woe is me, to be sad at heart!

IPHIGENIA Forbear; make me not a coward. Here in one thing obey me.

CLYTEMNESTRA Say what it is, my child, for at my hands thou shalt never suffer injury.

IPHIGENIA Cut not off the tresses of thy hair for me, nor clothe thyself in sable garb.

CLYTEMNESTRA Why, my child, What is it thou hast said? Shall I, when I lose thee—

IPHIGENIA "Lose" me thou dost not. I am saved and thou renowned, as far as I can make thee.

CLYTEMNESTRA How so? Must I not mourn thy death?

IPHIGENIA By no means, for I shall have no tomb heaped over me.

CLYTEMNESTRA What, is not the act of dying held to imply burial?

IPHIGENIA The altar of the goddess, Zeus' daughter, will be my tomb.

CLYTEMNESTRA Well, my child, I will let thee persuade me, for thou sayest well.

IPHIGENIA Aye, as one who prospereth and doeth Hellas service.

CLYTEMNESTRA What message shall I carry to thy sisters?

IPHIGENIA Put not mourning raiment on them either.

CLYTEMNESTRA But is there no fond message I can give the maidens from thee?

IPHIGENIA Yes, my farewell words; and promise me to rear this babe Orestes to manhood.

CLYTEMNESTRA Press him to thy bosom; 'tis thy last look.

IPHIGENIA Oh thou that art most dear to me! Thou hast helped thy friends as thou hadst means.

CLYTEMNESTRA Is there anything I can do to pleasure thee in Argos?

IPHIGENIA Yes, hate not my father, thy own husband.

CLYTEMNESTRA Fearful are the trials through which he has to go because of thee.

IPHIGENIA It was against his will he ruined me for the sake of Hellas.

CLYTEMNESTRA Ah! But he employed base treachery, unworthy of Atreus.

IPHIGENIA Who will escort me hence, before my hair is torn?

CLYTEMNESTRA I will go with thee.

IPHIGENIA No, not thou; thou say'st not well.

CLYTEMNESTRA I will, clinging to thy robes.

IPHIGENIA Be persuaded by me, Mother, stay here; for this is the better way alike for me and thee. Let one of these attendants of my father conduct me to the meadow of Artemis, where I shall be sacrificed.

CLYTEMNESTRA Art gone from me, my child?

IPHIGENIA Aye, and with no chance of ever returning.

CLYTEMNESTRA Leaving thy mother?

IPHIGENIA Yes, as thou seest, undeservedly.

CLYTEMNESTRA Hold! Leave me not!

IPHIGENIA I cannot let thee shed a tear.

Exit CLYTEMNESTRA

IPHIGENIA (*to the* CHORUS) Be it yours, maidens, to hymn in joyous strains Artemis, the child of Zeus, for my hard lot, and let the order for a solemn hush go forth to the Danai. Begin the sacrifice with the baskets, let the fire blaze for the purifying meal of sprinkling, and my father pace from left to right about the altar, for I come to bestow on Hellas safety crowned with victory. Lead me hence, me the destroyer of Ilium's town and the Phrygians. Give me wreaths to cast about me; bring them hither. Here are my tresses to crown; bring lustral water too. Dance to Artemis, Queen Artemis the blest, around her fane and altar; for by the blood of my sacrifice I will blot out the oracle, if it needs must be.

Oh Mother, lady revered! For thee shall my tears be shed, and now; for at the holy rites I may not weep.

Sing with me, maidens, sing the praises of Artemis, whose temple faces Chalcis, where angry spearmen madly chafe, here in the narrow havens of Aulis, because of me. Oh Pelasgia, land of my birth, and Mycenae, my home!

CHORUS Is it on Perseus' citadel thou callest, that town Cyclopean workmen build.

IPHIGENIA To be a light to Hellas didst thou rear me, and so I say not "No" to death.

CHORUS Thou art right; no fear that fame will ever desert thee!

IPHIGENIA Hail to thee, bright lamp of day and light of Zeus! A different life, different lot is henceforth mine. Farewell I bid thee, light beloved!

Exit IPHIGENIA

CHORUS Behold the maiden on her way, the destroyer of Ilium's town and its Phrygians, with garlands twined about her head, and drops of lustral water on her, soon to besprinkle with her gushing blood the altar of a murderous goddess, what time her shapely neck is severed.

For thee fair streams of a father's pouring and lustral waters are in store, for thee Achaea's host is waiting, eager to reach the citadel of Ilium. But let us celebrate Artemis, the daughter of Zeus, queen among the gods, as if upon some happy chance.

Oh lady revered, delighting in human sacrifice, send on its way to Phrygia's land the host of the Hellenes, to Troy's abodes of guile, and grant that Agamemnon may wreathe his head with deathless fame, a crown of fairest glory for the spearmen of Hellas.

Enter MESSENGER

MESSENGER Come forth, oh Clytemnestra, daughter of Tyndareus, from the tent to hear my news.

Enter CLYTEMNESTRA

CLYTEMNESTRA I heard thy voice and am come in sad dismay and fearful dread, not sure but what thou hast arrived with tidings of some fresh trouble for me besides the present woe.

MESSENGER Nay, rather would I unfold to thee a story strange and marvellous about thy child.

CLYTEMNESTRA Delay not then, but speak at once.

MESSENGER Dear mistress, thou shalt learn all clearly; from the outset will I tell it, unless my memory fail me somewhat and confuse my tongue in its account. As soon as we reached the grove of Artemis, the child of Zeus, and the meadows gay with flowers where the Achaean troops were gathered, bringing thy daughter with us, forthwith the Argive host began assembling. But when King Agamemnon saw the maiden on her way to the grove to be sacrificed, he gave one groan, and, turning away his face, let the tears burst from his eyes as he held his robe before them. But the maid, standing close by him that begot her, spake on this wise, "Oh my father, here am I to do thy bidding. Freely I offer this body of mine for my country and all Hellas, that ye may lead me to the altar of the goddess and sacrifice me, since this is Heaven's ordinance. Good luck be yours for any help that I afford! And may ye obtain the victor's gift and come again to the land of your fathers. So then let none of the Argives lay hands on me, for I will bravely yield my neck without a word."

She spake; and each man marvelled as he heard the maiden's brave, unflinching speech. But in the midst up stood Talthybius—for his this duty was—and bade the host refrain from word or deed; and Calchas the seer, drawing a sharp sword from out its scabbard laid it in a basket of beaten gold, crowning the maiden's head the while. Then the son of Peleus, taking the basket and with it lustral water in his hand, ran round the altar of the goddess uttering these words, "Oh Artemis, thou child of Zeus, slayer of wild beasts, that wheelest thy dazzling light amid the gloom, accept this sacrifice which we, the host of the Achaeans and King Agamemnon with us, offer to thee, even pure blood from a beauteous maiden's neck; and grant us safe sailing for our ships and the sack of Troy's towers by our spears."

Meantime the sons of Atreus and all the host stood looking on the ground, while the priest, seizing his knife, offered up a prayer and was closely scanning the maiden's throat to see where he should strike. 'Twas no slight sorrow filled my heart, as I stood by with bowed head, when lo! A sudden miracle! Each one of us distinctly heard the sound of a blow, but none saw the spot where the maiden vanished. Loudly the priest cried out, and all the host took up the cry at the sight of a marvel all unlooked for, due to some god's agency, and passing all belief, although 'twas seen. For there upon the ground lay a hind of size immense and passing fair to see, gasping out her life, with whose blood the altar of the goddess was thoroughly bedewed.

Whereon spake Calchas thus—his joy thou canst imagine—"Ye captains of this leagued Achaean host, do ye see this victim, which the goddess has set before her altar, a mountain roaming hind? This is more welcome to her by far than the maid, that she may not defile her altar by shedding noble blood. Gladly has she accepted it and is granting us a prosperous voyage for our attack on Ilium. Wherefore take heart, sailors, each man of you, and away to your ships, for today must we leave the hollow bays of Aulis and cross the Aegean main."

Then, when the sacrifice was wholly burnt to ashes in the blazing flame, he offered such prayers as were meet, that the army might win return; but me Agamemnon sends to tell thee this, and say what Heaven-sent luck is his, and how he hath secured undying fame throughout the length of Hellas. Now I was there myself and speak as an eye-witness: without a doubt thy child flew away to the gods. A truce then to thy sorrowing, and cease to be wroth with thy husband. For the gods' ways with man are not what we expect, and those whom they love they keepeth safe; yea, for this day hath seen thy daughter dead and brought to life again.

Exit MESSENGER

CHORUS What joy to hear these tidings from the messenger! He tells thee thy child is living still, among

119

the gods.

CLYTEMNESTRA Which of the gods, my child, hath stolen thee? How am I to address thee? How can I be sure that this is not an idle tale told to cheer me, to make me cease my piteous lamentation for thee?

CHORUS Lo! King Agamemnon approaches, to confirm this story for thee.

Enter AGAMEMNON

AGAMEMNON Happy may we be counted, lady, as far as concerns our daughter; for she hath fellowship with gods in very sooth. But thou must take this tender babe and start for home, for the host is looking now to sail. Fare thee well! 'Tis long ere I shall greet thee on my return from Troy; may it be well with thee!

CHORUS Son of Atreus, start for Phrygia's land with joy and so return, I pray, after taking from Troy her fairest spoils.

Exeunt OMNES

END

The Oenotropae

NOT many days after, with the armies having been set in order by the leaders and the perfect time for sailing now at hand, the ships were filled with all manner of costly goods which had been offered by the inhabitants of that region. As for grain, wine, and other necessary foodstuffs, all of this was provided by Anius and his daughters; these were known as the Oenotropae, and they were priestesses of a divine religion. In this way they sailed from Aulis.[10]

—Dictys Cretensis, *Ephemeris Belli Trojani*, I

VII.

Next they sail as far as Tenedos, and while they are feasting, Philoctetes is bitten by a snake and is left behind in Lemnos because of the stench of his sore. Here, too, Achilles quarrels with Agamemnon because he is invited late.

Then the Greeks tried to land at Ilium, but the Trojans prevent them, and Protesilaus is killed by Hector. Achilles then kills Cycnus, the son of Poseidon, and drives the Trojans back.

—Proclus, *Chrestomathy*

The Exile of Philoctetes

AFTER putting to sea from Aulis they touched at Tenedos. It was ruled by Tenes, son of Cycnus and Proclia, but according to some, he was a son of Apollo. He dwelt there because he had been banished by his father.

For Cycnus had a son Tenes and a daughter Hemithea by Proclia, daughter of Laomedon, but he afterwards married Philonome, daughter of Tragasus; and she fell in love with Tenes, and, failing to seduce him, falsely accused him to Cycnus of attempting to debauch her, and in witness of it she produced a flute-player, by name Eumolpus.

Cycnus believed her, and putting him and his sister in a chest he set them adrift on the sea. The chest was washed up on the island of Leucophrys, and Tenes landed and settled in the island, and called it Tenedos

122

after himself. But Cycnus afterwards learning the truth, stoned the flute-player to death and buried his wife alive in the earth.

So when the Greeks were standing in for Tenedos, Tenes saw them and tried to keep them off by throwing stones, but was killed by Achilles with a sword-cut in the breast, though Thetis had forewarned Achilles not to kill Tenes, because he himself would die by the hand of Apollo if he slew Tenes.

And as they were offering a sacrifice to Apollo, a water-snake approached from the altar and bit Philoctetes;[1] and as the sore did not heal and grew noisome, the army could not endure the stench, and Odysseus, by the orders of Agamemnon, put him ashore on the island of Lemnos, with the bow of Heracles which he had in his possession; and there, by shooting birds with the bow, he subsisted in the wilderness.

—Apollodorus, *Bibliotheca*, E.3.23-27

The Death of Protesilaus

THE Achaeans had been told by an oracle that he who first touched the shores of Troy would pay with his life. As the armada came to shore the Greeks held back, recalling the words of the oracle; all but Iolaus, son of Iphiclus and Diomedeae, who sprang forth from his ship and was quickly felled by Hector. He was afterwards called Protesilaus, because he was the first of them to be lost.[2]

When his wife, Laodamia daughter of Acastus, learned of his death, she wept and begged the gods that she be allowed to speak with her husband for three hours. Her prayer was answered, and Hermes led him back from the dead. But when their allotted three hours was spent and Protesilaus died for a second time, Laodamia was overcome by grief.

—Hyginus, *Fabulae*, CIII

The Grief of Laodamia

WHEN Laodamia the daughter of Acastus[3] had used up those three hours granted to her by the gods, she fell to weeping, unable to bear the loss she had endured. So she made herself a bronze statue of her husband Protesilaus which she kept in her chambers under the pretence that it was the statue of a god, and she began to worship it.

One morning a servant was bringing her fruits to be offered as a sacrifice, and peering through a crack in the door he saw Laodamia embracing and kissing the statue. Believing that she had taken a lover, he at once reported what he had seen to her father.

When Acastus entered the chamber he saw the image of Protesilaus. Wishing to end his daughter's torture, he commanded that the statue and the offerings be burned on a pyre. Laodamia, unable to bear her grief, threw herself upon the fire and was consumed by it.[4]

—Hyginus, *Fabulae*, CIV

Achilles and Cycnus

FAME now had spread the tidings, a great fleet of Greek ships was at that time on its way, an army of brave men. The Trojans stood, all ready to prevent the hostile

Greeks from landing on their shores. By the decree of Fate, the first man killed of the invaders' force was strong Protesilaus, by the spear of valiant Hector, whose unthought-of power at that time was discovered by the Greeks to their great cost.

The Phrygians also learned, at no small cost of blood, what warlike strength came from the Grecian land. The Sigean shores grew red with death-blood: Cycnus, Poseidon's son there slew a thousand men, for which, in wrath, Achilles pressed his rapid chariot straight through the Trojan army, making a lane with his great spear, shaped from a Pelion tree. And as he sought through the fierce battle's press—either for Cycnus or for Hector—he met Cycnus and engaged at once with him (fate had preserved great Hector from such foe till ten years from that day).

Cheering his steeds, their white necks pressed upon the straining yoke, he steered the chariot towards his foe, and, brandishing the spear with his strong arm, he cried, "Whoever you may be, you have the consolation of a glorious death; you die by me, Haemonian Achilles!"

His heavy spear flew after the fierce words. Although the spear was whirled direct and true, yet nothing it availed with sharpened point. It only bruised, as with a blunted stroke, the breast of Cycnus!

"By report we knew of you before this battle, goddess-born," the other answered him. "But why are you surprised that I escape the threatened wound?" Achilles was surprised. "This helmet crowned, great with its tawny horse-hair, and this shield, broad-hollowed, on my left arm, are not held for help in war; they are but ornament, as Ares wears armour. All of them shall be put off, and I will fight with you unhurt.

It is a privilege that I was born not as you, of a Nereid, but of him whose powerful rule is over Nereus, his daughters and their ocean." So he spoke.

Immediately he threw his spear against Achilles, destined to pierce the curving shield through brass and through nine folds of tough bull's hide. It stopped there, for it could not pierce the tenth. The hero wrenched it out, and hurled again a quivering spear at Cycnus, with great strength. The Trojan stood unwounded and unharmed. Nor did a third spear injure Cycnus, though he stood there with his body all exposed. Achilles raged at this, as a wild bull in open circus, when with dreadful horns he butts against the hanging purple robes which stir his wrath and there observes how they evade him, quite unharmed by his attack.

Achilles then examined his good spear, to see if by some chance the iron point was broken from it, but the point was firm, fixed on the wooden shaft. "My hand is weak," he said, "but is it possible its strength forsook me though it never has before? For surely I had my accustomed strength, when first I overthrew Lyrnessus' walls, or when I won the isle of Tenedos or Thebes (then under King Eetion) and I drenched both with their own peoples' blood, or when the river Caycus ran red with slaughter of its people,[5] or, when twice Telephus felt the virtue of my spear. On this field also, where such heaps lie slain, my right hand surely has proved its true might; and it is mighty." So he spoke of strength remembered.

But as if in proof against his own distrust, he hurled a spear against Menoetes, a soldier in the Lycian ranks. The sharp spear tore the victim's coat of mail and pierced his breast beneath. Achilles, when he saw his dying head strike on the earth wrenched the same spear from out the reeking wound, and said, "This is the hand, and this the spear I conquered with; and I will use the same against him who in luck escaped their power, and the result should favour as I pray the helpful gods." And, as he said such words, in haste he hurled his ashen spear, again at Cycnus. It went straight and struck un-shunned. Resounding on the shoulder of that foe, it bounced back as if it hit a wall or solid cliff. Yet when Achilles saw just where the spear struck Cycnus, there was stained with blood. He instantly rejoiced; but vainly, for it was Menoetes' blood!

Then in a sudden rage, Achilles leaped down headlong from his lofty chariot, and seeking his god-favoured foe, he struck in conflict fiercely with his gleaming sword. Although he saw that he had pierced both shield and helmet through, he did not harm the foe—his sword was even blunted on the flesh. Achilles could not hold himself for rage, but furious, with his sword-hilt and his shield he battered wildly the uncovered face and hollow temples of his Trojan foe. Cycnus gave way; Achilles rushed on him, buffeting fiercely, so that he could not recover from the shock.

Fear seized upon Cycnus, and darkness swam before his eyes. Then, as he moved back with retreating steps, a large stone hindered him and blocked his way. His back pushed against this, Achilles seized and dashed him violently to the ground. Then pressing with buckler and hard knees the breast of Cycnus, he unlaced the helmet thongs, wound them about the foeman's neck and drew them tightly under his chin, till Cycnus' throat could take no breath of life.

Achilles rose eager to strip his conquered foe but found his empty armour, for the god of ocean had changed the victim into that white bird whose name he lately bore.[6]

—Ovid, *Metamorphoses*, XII

WHEN the barbarians saw him dead they fled to the city, and the Greeks, leaping from their ships, filled the plain with bodies. And having shut up the Trojans, they besieged them; and they drew up the ships.

—Apollodorus, *Bibliotheca*, E.3.31

VIII.

The Greeks take up their dead and send envoys to the Tro-
jans demanding the surrender of Helen and the treasure with
her. The Trojans refusing, they first assault the city, and then
go out and lay waste the country and cities round about.
After this, Achilles desires to see Helen, and Aphrodite and
Thetis contrive a meeting between them.[1] *The Achaeans next*
desire to return home, but are restrained by Achilles, who
afterwards drives off the cattle of Aeneas, and sacks Lyrnes-
sus and Pedasus and many of the neighbouring cities, and
kills Troilus. Patroclus carries away Lycaon to Lemnos and
sells him as a slave, and out of the spoils Achilles receives
Briseis as a prize, and Agamemnon Chryseis.

—Proclus, *Chrestomathy*

The Greek Embassy

IT WAS decided that Odysseus and Diomedes would go
to Priam and attempt to persuade him to surrender
Helen and all of the wealth that had been seized. As
they made ready to leave Menelaus, who these negotia-
tions concerned, decided to join the delegation. In this
way they came to Troy.[2] As soon as the envoys arrived,
the Trojans, seeing that they were men of great promi-
nence, hastened to summon the elders and all of those
who occupied seats on the council. But Priam was kept
at home by his sons.

And so, in the presence of the council, Menelaus
decried the many wrongs that had been committed

against his house; with a groan, he complained that the absence of his wife had bereaved their daughter, and all of this from a former friend and guest who had no cause to mistreat him so. Hearing this the elders wept unrestrainedly, agreeing with all that he said as if they had suffered the injury themselves.

After that Odysseus stood up in their midst and addressed the council in this way: "I imagine that you, leaders of the Trojans, are quite aware that the Greeks will seldom begin anything rashly or without deliberation, and since the time of our ancestors have relied on careful planning, in order that our actions should garner praise rather than blame. And even so, having levied this army with many fine and celebrated generals, this war is not yet a foregone conclusion. In keeping with our usual practice of moderation, we now come to negotiate. The rest is in your hands, Trojans. We do not begrudge you this opportunity—if sounder heads may now prevail—to correct your previous ill-advised decisions.

"By the immortal gods, consider with all your hearts what disasters may spread throughout the world like a contagion. For who in the future, when entering vital negotiations, will not recall Paris' wickedness and view all of your motives with mistrust? Should brothers fear to welcome one another into their own homes? Who would not view his guest or his kinsman as a potential foe? In short, if you allow these things—and I dearly hope you will not—then friendship and accord between barbarian and Greek will be forever out of reach. Therefore, Trojan princes, it would be good and useful if the Greeks were to receive all the goods that have been wrested from them, and do not delay, lest the friendly relationship between our two kingdoms should turn to conflict.

"And by Heracles, when I consider your lot I feel sorrow, that those who are guiltless should suffer punishment for the crimes of a few. For if Helen and all that was stolen is not restored to us, then war cannot be averted; a war that will not end until all of the Greek leaders—each one capable of taking this city—lie dead, or else, as is my I hope, the city of Ilium is captured and burned, with only its ashes left for posterity as an example of your impiety. For this reason I ask you: while the power yet lies in your hands, prevent this."

When he had finished speaking there was a great silence, as is common at such times when every man waits to hear the opinion of others, regarding his own as inferior, until Panthus said in a loud voice: "Odysseus, you are addressing those who have not the power to remedy these matters."

Then after spake Antenor: "All these things which have been mentioned by you are true, and had we the authority we would do what is wise and prudent. But, as you can see, power is wielded by those with interests contrary to the welfare of our people." Having made his argument, he immediately ordered that all of the leaders who had come because of friendship with Priam, as well as all who had been hired as mercenaries and auxiliaries, should now be introduced.

As these arrived Odysseus began a second oration, calling them the most iniquitous of men; no different from Paris, the most heinous of criminals, having deserted all things good and honourable in following him.

None were ignorant of the fact that if they approved of such a terrible injustice, it would set an evil example that would be disseminated throughout the nearby peoples, spreading fear among neighbouring kingdoms that similar or more serious evil might follow. All these hideous things they silently considered amongst themselves, being moved to indignation by their own culpability. Then in their customary way the elders put forth the motion that Menelaus had suffered an injurious wrong, and the decree was passed, with Antimachus alone taking Paris' part, in opposition to all. And at once two men were chosen, and commanded to report all of these things to Priam.

When the king received this news he was greatly distraught, and right before their eyes he collapsed. After a moment he was revived, with those that stood by helping him to his feet, and he would have gone to the council had they not restrained him. Now having left their father the sons of Priam rushed to the council, where up to that time Antimachus had been railing against the Greeks and their threats, and suggesting that Menelaus ought to be detained as a hostage.[3] His proposal had been met with silence, with only Antenor speaking out, stating that he would resist any such decree with all of his power. After this the pair engaged in a fierce debate, until, having expended all speech they came to blows. And all who were present pronounced Antimachus to be unruly and seditious, and banished him from the council.

But when the sons of Priam entered, Panthus begged Hector—for among the princes he was held to be the most wise and virtuous—that Helen, especially now that the Greeks had come as suppliants, be amicably restored to them. Never mind Paris' love for Helen, which he had had ample time to enjoy. With things being as they were, they must detain the envoys no longer and allow them to depart with Helen, pledging friendship and union between the two kingdoms.

Upon hearing this Hector was moved to tears, recalling his brother's crime. However, he did not agree that Helen should be returned, for she had come into their house as a suppliant, and as such was under their protection. But were they to describe those items which had been taken with her, these he would gladly restore. And in the place of Helen, Cassandra or Polyxena— whomever seemed best to the envoys—would be given in marriage to Menelaus along with many splendid gifts.

At this, Menelaus was enraged: "By Heracles, what a noble act is this," he cried, "if the one despoiled of his wife should be forced into another marriage according to the will of his enemies!"

Then Aeneas spoke against him: "You would not even be conceded this," he said, "were it up to me, for I oppose it, as do all the friends and kinsmen of Paris who give him counsel. For there are and always shall be those sworn to protect the house and kingdom of Priam. Are only those who come from Greece permitted to commit such rape? The Cretans who seized Europa from Sidon, and Ganymede from our lands. And what of Medea? You cannot be ignorant of how she was carried off from Colchis all the way to Iolcus. And not to forget the first rape of all, when Io was abducted from the land of the Sidonians and carried to Argos.[4] But thus far we have been talking in circles. If you do not take your ships and promptly flee these lands you will experience Trojan might, for here we have an abundance of young men who are skilled in war, and our auxiliaries increase in number with each passing day."

And when he had finished his speech, Odysseus calmly said: "Then by Heracles, delay not these hostilities any longer. Give the signal for war; let those who first inflicted the injury also commence the battle. We will await your attack." Following this exchange the envoys left the council.

Soon after, word spread among the people of how Aeneas had spoken against the envoys, and they raised a mighty tumult; they believed he was the reason why the house of Priam was universally hated, and that his blundering intervention would see the kingdom overthrown.

—Dictys Cretensis, *Ephemeris Belli Trojani*, II

The Burning of Neandreia

FIRSTLY, the Greeks sent a detachment from the main army to ravage the kingdoms around Troy. Thus they invaded the country of Cycnus, and despoiled the surrounding lands. But when they set fire to the city of Neandreia, which was the capital of Cycnus' kingdom and also where his sons were being raised, the citizens offered no resistance to the invasion. With many prayers and tears they went down on their knees and begged the Greeks, by all things human and divine, to spare their city; its citizens were innocent of the sins of its leader, and were ready to bend the knee. Thus mercy was shown, and the city saved.

However, the Greeks did require that the royal sons Cobis and Corianus and their sister Glauce be turned over to them; Glauce was given to Ajax in addition to the rest of his booty, on account of his mighty deeds.

Not long after, the Neandreians came as suppliants to the Greeks, asking for peace and friendship, promising to do as they commanded. This done, the Greeks now attacked and destroyed Cilla. But they did not sack Carene, which was not far distant, out of respect for their new-found allies the Neandreians, who were lords of that city.

In the meantime Achilles, believing that some of the cities near to Troy were supplying them with weapons and soldiers, set off for Lesbos with a number of ships and took the island without difficulty. He slew Phorbas, the king of that land, who had committed many hostile acts against the Greeks, and captured Diomedea, daughter of the king, along with a great quantity of plunder.

—Dictys Cretensis, *Ephemeris Belli Trojani*, II

Achilles and Trambelus

TRAMBELUS the son of Telamon fell in love with a girl named Apriate in Lesbos. He used every effort to gain her: but, as she shewed no signs at all of relenting, he determined to win her by strategy and guile. She was walking one day with her attendant handmaids to one of her father's domains which was by the seashore, and there he laid an ambush for her and made her captive; but she struggled with the greatest violence to protect her virginity, and at last Trambelus in fury threw her into the sea, which happened at that point to be deep inshore.

Thus did she perish; the story has, however, been related by others in the sense that she threw herself in while fleeing from his pursuit. It was not long before divine vengeance fell upon Trambelus: Achilles was ravaging Lesbos and carrying away great quantities of booty, and Trambelus got together a company of the inhabitants of the island, and went out to meet him in battle. In the course of it he received a wound in the breast and instantly fell to the ground; while he was still breathing, Achilles, who had admired his valour, inquired of his name and origin.

When he was told that he was the son of Telamon, he bewailed him long and deeply, and piled up a great barrow for him on the beach: it is still called "the hero Trambelus' mound."[5]

—Parthenius, *Love Romances*, XXVI

Briseis and Chryseis

THEN on to Skyros[6] and Hierapolis, both cities filled with riches, which he attacked with great force and easily conquered and razed within a few days.

Every place Achilles went fell under his yoke; he plundered them all, spreading terror throughout the region. Any settlements that seemed friendly to Troy were stripped and laid waste. The other neighbouring peoples, being informed of what was happening, now hurried to make treaties with him to prevent the desolation of their own lands. They promised to give half of their harvest in return for peace, and to this he agreed. With these acts Achilles re-joined the army in great glory, bringing much plunder. At the same time the king of the Scythians, having learned of the Greeks' arrival, came bearing many gifts.

But Achilles—not content with these deeds—now attacked the Cilicians, and after a few days of fighting he captured the city of Lyrnessus. Having slain Eetion, who was the ruler of that land, he filled his ships with a great amount of booty, and also abducted Chryseis, who was the daughter of Chryses and at that time the king's wife.[7]

Then he promptly moved on to conquer Pedasus, city of the Leleges. When their king, Brises, observed the ferocity of the siege, he realised they would not be able to mount a sufficient defence. With no hope of escape or salvation, he returned to his home while the rest of his men fought on, and hanged himself. Not long after the city was taken, with many of its people slain, as well as the capture of the king's daughter, Briseis.[8]

During the same time Telamonian Ajax went to the country of the Phrygians, and entering the kingdom of Teuthras he slew him in single combat.[9] After a few days he captured and burned the city, carrying away a vast quantity of plunder and abducting Tecmessa, daughter of the king.

Now both of these leaders, having conquered and laid waste to many regions and performed mighty deeds, re-joined the army together as if by design, although they came from different directions. Then when the heralds had gathered together all of the soldiers and generals, they advanced into their midst one by one, displaying to all the fruits of their labour and industry. When the Greeks saw what they had captured they showered them with praise, and as the two heroes stood among them they were crowned with olive branches.

Then when it came to dividing the spoils they consulted Nestor and Idomeneus, who were held to be the most wise and discerning among them. And so, without delay, judgement was made upon the spoils that Achilles had brought, with Chryseis, the wife of Eetion and daughter of Chryses, given to Agamemnon on account of his royal standing. To Achilles went Briseis, daughter of Brises, and he also retained Diomedea; given their similarities in age and upbringing it would have caused them great suffering were they to be parted. Indeed, they had gone down on their knees before Achilles and begged not to be separated. The rest of the spoils were distributed amongst the men according to merit.

Then Ajax asked Odysseus and Diomedes to bring forth the plunder that he had won. From this, gold and silver were given to Agamemnon, in sufficient quantity as befitted his status as king; then to Ajax, as a reward for his outstanding deeds and toil, they conceded Tecmessa, the daughter of Teuthras.

Then the remaining spoils were divided among the others, and the grain distributed throughout the army.

—Dictys Cretensis, *Ephemeris Belli Trojani*, II

The Death of Troilus and the Cattle of Aeneas

THE barbarians showing no courage, Achilles waylaid Troilus and slaughtered him in the sanctuary of Thymbraean Apollo,[10] and coming by night to the city he captured Lycaon. Moreover, taking some of the chiefs with him, Achilles laid waste the country, and made his way to Ida to lift the kine of Aeneas. But Aeneas fled, and Achilles killed the neatherds and Nestor, son of Priam, and drove away the kine.[11]

—Apollodorus, *Bibliotheca*, E.3.32

The Capture of Lycaon

A SON of Dardanian Priam ... even Lycaon [was] taken from his father's orchard ... in the night; he was cutting with the sharp bronze the young shoots of a wild fig-tree, to be the rims of a chariot; but upon him, an unlooked-for bane, came godly Achilles. For that time had he sold him into well-built Lemnos, bearing him thither on his ships, and the son of Jason had given a price for him;[12] but from thence a guest-friend had ransomed him—and a great price he gave—even Eetion of Imbros, and had sent him unto goodly Arisbe; whence he ... fled forth secretly and [returned] to the house of his fathers.[13]

—Homer, *Iliad*, XXI

IX.

Then follows the death of Palamedes, the plan of Zeus to relieve the Trojans by detaching Achilles from the Hellenic confederacy, and a catalogue of the Trojan allies.

—Proclus, Chrestomathy

The Murder of Palamedes

ODYSSEUS, because his deceit had been undermined by Palamedes son of Nauplius, now plotted to be rid of him. At last he formed a plan, and sent one of his soldiers to Agamemnon, saying that he had seen in a dream that the camp must be moved for a single day. Supposing it to be true, Agamemnon gave the command that the camp should be moved for one day. That night Odysseus secretly hid a great amount of gold where the tent of Palamedes had been, and also gave a letter to a Phrygian prisoner for the hand of Priam. He then instructed one of his soldiers to kill the prisoner only a short distance from the camp.

On the following day, when the men returned to the camp, a certain soldier discovered the dead body of the Phrygian, on whom was placed the letter which Odysseus had written, and brought it to Agamemnon. In it was written: "TO PALAMEDES FROM PRIAM", along with the promise of gold—as much as had been hidden in the tent—if he would betray the camp of Agamemnon as they had agreed.

140

Palamedes, when he was hauled before the king, denied the charge. But when they went to his tent and discovered the gold, Agamemnon believed it to be true. Thus Palamedes was ensnared by Odysseus, and the entire army was deceived into killing an innocent man.[1]

—Hyginus, *Fabulae*, CV

Catalogue of the Trojan Allies

DURING same time, at Troy, the army of allies and mercenaries who had been hired as auxiliary troops—perhaps due to frustration and tedium, or a yearning for their homelands—now began to mutiny. On perceiving this, Hector was compelled by necessity to muster his soldiers; to have them armed, and thus ready to follow when the signal was given. So when, having received reports that the time was ripe and his men were all in arms, he ordered them to march; himself the leader and commander of the army.

It now seems fitting to list the kings of the allies and friends of Troy, as well as those mercenaries and auxiliaries from various regions who had been hired by the sons of Priam to defend the kingdom.[2] The first to charge from the city gates was Pandarus the son of Lycaon, from Lycia; then Hippothous and Pylaeus from Pelasgian Larissa; Acamas and Peirous of Thrace; and after them Euphemus son of Troezenus, leading the Ciconians. There was boastful Pylaemenes of Paphlagonia, whose father was Melius; Odius and Epistrophus, sons of Minuus, the Halizonian king; Sarpedon born of Xanthus,[3] leader of the Lycians, from Solymum; Nastes and Amphimachus, sons of Noimon from Caria; and Antiphus and Mesthles, whose sire was

141

Talaemenes, from Maeonia. Then Glaucus son of Hippolochus, of Lycia, chosen by Sarpedon to be his second-in-command because he stood above all others in counsel and deeds of arms; Phorcys and Ascanius of Phrygia; Chromius and Ennomus, Mygdonians from Mysia; and Pyraechmes son of Axius, from Paeonia;[4] Amphius and Adrastus, born of Merops, from Adrestia; Asius son of Hyrtacus, from Sestos. Then the other Asius, Dymas' son and brother of Hecuba, from Phrygia. All of these listed were followed by many men of disparate customs and languages, which caused them to go into battle without any order.

When the Greeks took notice of this, they advanced onto the field and formed a battle line under the direction of Menestheus, the Athenian, organised according to their various tribes and regions. Now, having deployed their army, they were for the first time preparing to engage the full might of the enemy, yet neither side dared to commit; each stood their ground for a time, until—as though by mutual agreement—both sides sounded the retreat.

—Dictys Cretensis, *Ephemeris Belli Trojani*, II

With this account of the Trojan allies the story of the *Cypria* comes to a close, and we are now ready for Homer to pick up the tale:

The Wrath of Achilles

THE wrath sing, goddess, of Peleus' son, Achilles, that destructive wrath which brought countless woes upon the Achaeans, and sent forth to Hades many valiant souls of heroes, and made them themselves spoil for dogs and every bird; thus the plan of Zeus came to fulfilment, from the time when first they parted in strife Atreus' son, king of men, and brilliant Achilles...

—Homer, *Iliad*, I

NOTES

I.

1. Titaness of law and social order. Aeschylus also made her the mother of Prometheus (*Prometheus Bound*, ll. 217-219), although Prometheus is more commonly said to have been the son of the Titan Iapetus and the sea nymph Clymene.

2. Hesiod offered another motive. Zeus had decided that gods should no longer mate with mortals, and wished to "destroy the race of demi-gods", i.e. the descendants of gods and mortals (*Catalogue of Women*, Fragment 68, II, ll. 2-13).

3. "The author of the *Cypria* says that Thetis, to please Hera, avoided union with Zeus, at which he was enraged and swore that she should be the wife of a mortal." (*Volumina Herculan,* II. VIII. 105)

4. In Apollodorus' *Bibliotheca* it is Chiron who tells Peleus how to capture Thetis (III.13.5).

5. "For at the marriage of Peleus and Thetis, the gods gathered together on Pelion to feast and brought Peleus gifts. Chiron gave him a stout ashen shaft which he had cut for a spear, and Athena, it is said, polished it, and Hephaestus fitted it with a head. The story is given by the author of the *Cypria*." (Scholiast on Homer, *Iliad*, XVII)

6. A lost section of the *Aegimius*, a fragmentary poem attributed to Hesiod, contained a slightly different version of the myth: "Thetis used to throw the children she had by Peleus into a cauldron of water, because she wished to learn where they were mortal ... And that after many had perished Peleus was annoyed, and prevented her from throwing Achilles into the cauldron." (Scholiast on Apollonius Rhodius, *Argonautica*, Book IV) The myth of the infant

144

Achilles being dipped in the river Styx, rendering his body impervious to weapons apart from where Thetis had gripped his heel, is relatively late. It first appears in the unfinished epic *Achilleid* (c. 95 AD) by the Roman poet Statius.

7. *A-* = not/an absence of, *cheilê* = lips. This etymology is probably incorrect, with Achilles' name commonly translated as *ákhos* = sorrow, *laos* = host or army.

8. *Alexô* = to defend, *andros* = man.

9. Paris' first marriage to the nymph Oenone is not mentioned in the *Excidium Troiae* or Colluthus' *Rape of Helen*. Her prophecy is realised in Quintus Smyrnaeus' *Posthomerica* when Paris, mortally wounded by the arrow of Philoctetes, returns to her and begs that she heal him. She refuses, but after his death is overcome by remorse and commits suicide (X.272-519). Note that Paris was not the only son of Priam to marry a daughter of Cebren (see p. 4).

10. Peitho or "Persuasion" was an attendant goddess of Aphrodite. Hesiod made her the daughter of the Titans Oceanus and Tethys (*Theogony*, 349), but she was more commonly said to be a daughter of Aphrodite, with Dionysus sometimes named as her father.

11. The Loves or "Erotes" were the winged love gods who formed Aphrodite's retinue, including Eros (Cupid), Anteros, Hedylogos, Pothos, Himeros, Hermaphroditus and Hymen. Most were the children of Aphrodite and Ares, or Hermes (Hermaphroditus), or Dionysus (Hymen). Originally depicted as winged youths, in Roman and later art they were represented as cherubs.

12. A cattle prod (archaic).

13. "The author of the *Cypria*, whether Hegesias or Stasinus, mentions flowers used for garlands. The poet, whoever he was, writes as follows in his first book: 'She clothed herself with garments which the Graces and Hours had made for her and dyed in flowers of spring—such flowers as the Seasons wear—in crocus and hyacinth and flourishing violet and the rose's lovely bloom, so sweet and delicious, and heavenly buds, the flowers of the narcissus and lily. In such perfumed garments is Aphrodite clothed at all seasons. [Lacuna] Then laughter-loving Aphrodite and her handmaidens

wove sweet-smelling crowns of flowers of the earth and put them upon their heads—the bright-coiffed goddesses, the Nymphs and Graces, and golden Aphrodite too, while they sang sweetly on the mount of many-fountained Ida.'" (Athenaeus, XV. 682 D, F)

14. A war goddess, and sister or companion/consort of Ares. In the *Iliad* Homer identifies her with Eris, although most writers distinguished between the two; Eris (Strife) was not exclusively a war goddess, representing discord and general mayhem as opposed to actual combat.

II.

1. A quote from Herodotus contradicts this: "For it is said in the *Cypria* that Paris came with Helen to Ilium from Sparta in three days, enjoying a favourable wind and calm sea." (Herodotus, II. 117)

2. Apollodorus gave Tyndareus and Leda two other daughters: Philonoe and Timandra. Philonoe was made immortal by Artemis, and Timandra was married to King Echemus of Arcadia, whom she later deserted for Phyleus, father of Meges (*Bibliotheca*, III.10.6). According to Euripides' *Iphigenia at Aulis* (l. 50) and Ovid (*Heroides*, 8.77), Helen and Clytemnestra had only one sister: Phoebe. If there were any myths associated with her they have not survived.

3. "And after them she bare a third child, Helen, a marvel to men. Rich-tressed Nemesis once gave her birth when she had been joined in love with Zeus the king of the gods by harsh violence. For Nemesis tried to escape him and liked not to lie in love with her father Zeus the Son of Cronus; for shame and indignation vexed her heart: therefore she fled him over the land and fruitless dark water. But Zeus ever pursued and longed in his heart to catch her. Now she took the form of a fish and sped over the waves of the loud-roaring sea, and now over Ocean's stream and the furthest bounds of Earth, and now she sped over the furrowed land, always turning into such dread creatures as the dry land nurtures, that she might

escape him." (Athenaeus, VIII. 334 B) According to Philodemus' *On Piety* (c. 50 BC), the story of Helen being born from an egg was also told in the *Cypria*.

4. "For Helen had been previously carried off by Theseus, and it was in consequence of this earlier rape that Aphidna, a town in Attica, was sacked and Castor was wounded in the right thigh by Aphidnus who was king at that time. Then the Dioscuri, failing to find Theseus, sacked Athens. The story is in the Cyclic writers." (Scholiast on Homer, *Iliad*, III) "Hereas relates that Alycus was killed by Theseus himself near Aphidna, and quotes the following verses in evidence: 'In spacious Aphidna Theseus slew him in battle long ago for rich-haired Helen's sake.'" (Plutarch, *Theseus*, 32). Hereas is an unknown writer. The quote, describing the death of a companion of Castor and Pollux, is presumed to be from the *Cypria*.

5. Hyginus adds Ancaeus son of Poseidon, Blanirus, Clytius of Cyane, Idomeneus of Crete, Meriones, Nireus son of Charopus, Phemius, Phidippus son of Thessalus, Prothous son of Tenthredon, Thoas son of Andraemon, and Tlepolemus son of Heracles (*Fabulae*, 81).

6. Icarius was the brother of Tyndareus, making Helen and Penelope first cousins.

7. Demophon was the son of Theseus, who along with his brother Acamas went to Troy to rescue their grandmother Aethra. Here Colluthus makes reference to the myth of Demophon and Phyllis; unusually, as their encounter is said to have occurred after the Trojan War, so Paris could not have seen Phyllis' tomb: "Demophon with a few ships put in to the land of the Thracian Bisaltians, and there Phyllis, the king's daughter, falling in love with him, was given him in marriage by her father with the kingdom for her dower. But he wished to depart to his own country, and after many entreaties and swearing to return, he did depart. And Phyllis accompanied him as far as what are called the Nine Roads, and she gave him a casket, telling him that it contained a sacrament of Mother Rhea, and that he was not to open it until he should have abandoned all hope of returning to her. And Demophon went to

Cyprus and dwelt there. And when the appointed time was past, Phyllis called down curses on Demophon and killed herself; and Demophon opened the casket, and, being struck with fear, he mounted his horse and galloping wildly met his end; for, the horse stumbling, he was thrown and fell on his sword." (Apollodorus, *Bibliotheca,* E.6.16-17)

8. Book X of Ovid's *Metamorphoses* tells the story of Hyacinthus in greater detail. Hyacinthus was the mortal companion of Apollo, accidentally slain by the latter during a game of discus. As he died, a hyacinth flower sprouted where his blood had spilled onto the earth.

9. Here Menelaus is apparently already in Crete when Paris arrives. From Proclus, we know that in the *Cypria* Menelaus entertained Paris before his departure. Colluthus also omits Paris' sojourn with Castor and Pollux.

10. Some (non-Homeric) sources also gave Menelaus and Helen at least one son, Nicostratus, although in the *Cypria* they evidently had two: "The writer of the Cyprian Histories says that [Helen's third child was] Pleisthenes and that she took him with her to Cyprus, and that the child she bore Paris was Aganus." (Scholiast on Euripides, *Andromache*)

11. This version of events, which does not appear in the Epic Cycle, forms the subject of Euripides' *Helen.*

12. *Diós* = Zeus, *Kouros* = youth or boy. Sir James George Frazer interpreted *Dioscuri* as "striplings of Zeus".

13. "Straightway Lynceus, trusting in his swift feet, made for Taygetus. He climbed its highest peak and looked throughout the whole isle of Pelops, son of Tantalus; and soon the glorious hero with his dread eyes saw horse-taming Castor and athlete Pollux both hidden within a hollow oak." (Scholiast on Pindar, *Nemean Ode X*) "[Stasinus?] writes that Castor was killed with a spear shot by Idas the son of Aphareus." (Philodemus, *On Piety*)

14. Here it is Zeus, and not Pollux (as per the *Chrestomathy*) who kills Idas.

15. "Castor was mortal, and the fate of death was destined for him; but Pollux, scion of Ares, was immortal." (Clement of Alexan-

dria, *Protrept*) "Scion of Ares" is meant figuratively, alluding to his martial prowess. Interestingly, the *Iliad* seems to treat both Castor and Pollux as dead: in Book III, when Helen looks down upon the Greek armies from the walls of Troy, she wonders why she cannot see her brothers, not knowing that they "were fast holden of the life-giving earth there in Lacedaemon, in their dear native land." *Odyssey* XI on the other hand acknowledges their partial immortality; this is sometimes held up as evidence that it was the work of a different poet.

III.

1. Dictys has here confused Atreus son of Pelops with Catreus son of Minos—it is in fact Catreus who has died. This possibly arose due to Agamemnon and Menelaus' descent from both men; Catreus was their maternal grandfather.

2. Deucalion was a son of Minos; Molus was the illegitimate son of Deucalion, and thus half-brother to Idomeneus.

3. Clymene, mother of Palamedes, was the daughter of Catreus.

4. In Homer's *Odyssey* the wife of Nestor is Eurydice, daughter of Clymenus. Other sources record Anaxibia as the wife of Strophius, king of Phocis; their son was Pylades, cousin and companion to Orestes in Aeschylus' *Oresteia*.

5. Pleisthenes was the son of Atreus; thus, Agamemnon and Menelaus were fostered by their grandfather. This detail appeared in Hesiod (Tzetzes, *Exegesis of the Iliad*, 68. 19H), but not Homer, in which they are only ever referred to as the sons of Atreus.

6. Europa was the mother of King Minos, seduced by Zeus when he took the form of a white bull.

7. According to Pausanias, the *Cypria* was unique in making Eurydice the wife of Aeneas, rather than Creusa, daughter of Priam (*Description of Greece*, 10.26.1).

8. Dictys seems to be unaware that although Aethra and her daughter Clymene were indeed Menelaus' kinswomen (Aethra's father Pittheus was the brother of Atreus), they were also his slaves,

captured by the Dioscuri when they recovered Helen from Athens.

9. The *Chrestomathy* has Nestor tell the story of Epopeus "seducing the daughter of Lycus", but Antiope is usually said to have been the daughter of Nycetus, brother of Lycus. It is conceivable that this represents an error on Proclus' part, rather than an alternate parentage (as interpreted by some scholars).

10. Cowherd (archaic).

11. *Oideo* = to swell, *pous* = foot.

12. It is unlikely that Nestor spoke of Heracles without mentioning the fact that he killed his father and eleven brothers: "[Heracles] I recall once overthrew Messene's walls and with no cause destroyed Elis and Pylos and with fire and sword ruined my own loved home. I cannot name all whom he killed. But there were twelve of us, the sons of Neleus and all warrior youths, and all those twelve but me alone he killed." (Ovid, *Metamorphoses*, XII)

13. The "clue" was a ball of thread.

IV.

1. The horse and ox would move at different speeds; hence one would be mad to yoke them together. Some later sources add that Odysseus sowed the field with salt.

2. Eustathius of Thessalonica (c. 1115 - 1195/6AD) writes that Cinyras was cursed by Agamemnon, and later slain by Apollo after losing a contest to see who was the more skilled at playing the lyre. Upon his death, Cinyras' fifty daughters threw themselves into the sea and were transformed into sea birds (*Commentary on Iliad XI*). Ovid tells a different version of the myth, where his daughter Myrrha conceives an unnatural lust for her father and tricks him into having intercourse. Upon discovering her identity Cinyras attempts to kill her, but she flees from him and is transformed into a myrrh tree by the gods. The myrrh tree later gives birth to Adonis, although in Greek versions of the Adonis myth Myrrha was the daughter of Theias of Assyria (*Metamorphoses*, X).

3. According to Hyginus, Achilles was known as "Pyrrha" to the

women of Lycomedes' court due to his red hair, *pyrrhos* meaning red in Greek. This physical trait he shared with his son, Pyrrhus being the masculine form. Pausanias, in his *Description of Greece* (10.26.4), writes that in the *Cypria* Lycomedes gave his grandson the name Pyrrhus, and Phoenix named him Neoptolemus because Achilles was young when he went to war (*neo* = new, *pólemos* = war).

4. According to a scholiast on the *Iliad*, the "Cyclic writers" gave a slightly different account of Achilles at Skyros. He was hidden there by Peleus at the outbreak of the war, and Odysseus, Phoenix and Nestor were sent to recruit him. Suspecting that Achilles was disguised among the girls, Odysseus had them spread a quantity of weapons along with some baskets and weaving implements in front of the girls' chambers. When Achilles showed interest in the weapons, he was discovered. In Ovid's *Metamorphoses*, Odysseus describes it similarly during the contest for Achilles' arms, although he adds that Telamonian Ajax was also present: "Achilles' Nereid mother, who foresaw his death, concealed her son by change of dress. By that disguise Ajax, among the rest, was well-deceived. I showed with women's wares arms that might win the spirit of a man. The hero still wore clothing of a girl, when, as he held a shield and spear, I said 'Son of a goddess! Pergama but waits to fall by you, why do you hesitate to assure the overthrow of mighty Troy?'" (Ovid, *Metamorphoses*, XIII)

5. "It should be observed that the ancient narrative hands down the account that Patroclus was even a kinsman of Achilles; for Hesiod says that Menoetius the father of Patroclus, was a brother of Peleus, so that in that case they were first cousins." (Eustathius, commentary on Homer's *Iliad*)

6. Daughter of Ares and Aphrodite, and goddess of marriage.

7. Presumably the heir of the Sidonian king lately murdered by Paris.

V.

1. This catalogue largely agrees with the one found in *Iliad* II, although Homer arrives at 1,186 ships. Hyginus lists 1,154, and divides the army into 46 contingents (*Fabulae*, 97).

2. According to Apollodorus, it took two years for the Greek armies to actually muster (*Bibliotheca*, E.3.18). If we assume that Achilles was born in the year after the wedding of Peleus and Thetis, then some thirteen years must have elapsed between Paris' judgement of the goddesses and his abduction of Helen.

3. Here there is no mention of the Greeks mistaking the city of Teuthrania for Troy as in the *Chrestomathy*.

4. Polynices and Tydeus, the fathers of Thersander and Diomedes, were two of the Seven Against Thebes. A decade later Thersander and Diomedes joined the Epigoni ("offspring") who returned to Thebes to avenge their fathers: "The men who took part in the expedition were these: Alcmaeon and Amphilochus, sons of Amphiaraus; Aegialeus, son of Adrastus; Diomedes, son of Tydeus; Promachus, son of Parthenopaeus; Sthenelus, son of Capaneus; Thersander, son of Polynices; and Euryalus, son of Mecisteus." (Apollodorus, *Bibliotheca*, III.7.2). Of these, Amphilochus, Diomedes, Sthenelus, Thersander and Euryalus all fought in the Trojan War.

5. Heracles' mother Alcmene was sometimes said to be the daughter or granddaughter of Pelops

6. According to Philostratus (c. 170 to 250 AD), the wife of Telephus was Hiera. She was slain by Nireus of Syme whilst leading the Mysian cavalry against the Greek invaders (*On Heroes*, II.23.27). This episode is also depicted on the Pergamon Altar, which dates from the 2nd century BC. Telephus' son Eurypylus appeared in the *Little Iliad*, one of the lost Cyclic Epics, joining the war on the side of the Trojans after the death of Achilles. He killed a number of Greeks, including Machaon the son of Asclepius, before dying at the hands of Neoptolemus. The story is retold in Quintus Smyrnaeus' *Posthomerica*, Books VI-VIII.

7. This friendly exchange is probably unique to Dictys; other ac-

counts placed Telephus' reconciliation with the Greeks after the healing of his wound at Argos. Proclus seems to imply that in the *Cypria* Telephus fled after his wounding and did not reencounter the Greeks until his appearance at Argos, but it is impossible to know what has been omitted.

8. In Euripides' *Telephus*, a lost play of the 5th century BC, Telephus kidnapped the infant Orestes and threatened to slay him if Achilles did not heal the wound. This is also the version given by Hyginus (*Fabulae* 101).

VI.

1. Contrast with Apollodorus' version in Chapter I, where the oath is suggested by Odysseus.

2. The Classical Greeks believed that the city of Mycenae had been built by the Cyclopes, due to the enormous stone blocks used in its construction; hence the term "Cyclopean" to describe such masonry.

3. Euripides here conflates Nauplius son of Poseidon with Nauplius son of Clytoneus, father of Palamedes and member of the Argonauts. Many writers—Apollodorus and Hyginus included—made the same error, but the father of Palamedes was in fact the great-great-grandson of the earlier Nauplius.

4. A figure of speech. Meriones was the son of Molus, the half-brother of Idomeneus (see III note 2).

5. The rumour that Sisyphus, famously condemned to push a boulder up a hill for all eternity, was the true father of Odysseus is not found in Homer, or (presumably) the other Cyclic Epics. Its earliest known appearance is in Sophocles' *Ajax*, written in the latter half of the 5th century BC.

6. Cypris = Aphrodite. "Lady of Cypris", where she is often said to have been born.

7. Most accounts give Agamemnon and Clytemnestra three daughters: Iphigenia, Chrysothemis and Electra (Laodice in the *Iliad*). Some versions, including the *Cypria*, added a fourth: "Either

he follows Homer who spoke of the three daughters of Agamem-
non, or—like the writer of the *Cypria*—he makes them four, [distin-
guishing] Iphigenia and Iphianassa." (Laurentian scholiast on
Sophocles, *Electra*)

8. Inachus was the first king of Argos; i.e. Iphigenia should have
grown up to one day be wedded to an Argive prince.

9. Clytemnestra's warning of course foreshadows the eventual
murder of Agamemnon upon his return from Troy. In Aeschylus'
Agamemnon he dies by the hand of Clytemnestra herself; in the
Odyssey the murder is said to have been committed by Clytemnes-
tra's lover (and Agamemnon's cousin) Aegisthus, who afterwards
usurped the throne of Mycenae until he was slain in turn by Ores-
tes.

10. This is a somewhat mangled version of the Oenotropae myth,
which is known to have appeared at some point in the *Cypria* from
a scholiast on Lycophron's *Alexandra*. The three daughters of King
Anius of Delos (Dictys places them at Aulis, which is nowhere near
Delos), known as the Oenotropae, were granted the power of
producing oil, corn and wine from the earth by Dionysus. At some
point in their voyage to Troy the Greeks landed at Delos, and Anius
offered to let them stay there and be fed by his daughters for nine
years, knowing that Troy would not be taken until the tenth. Later,
while the Greeks were besieging the city, Agamemnon had Pala-
medes fetch the Oenotropae to keep his armies from starving.
According to Ovid's *Metamorphoses*, Agamemnon brought them to
Troy by force; they escaped to Andros, and when the Greeks caught
up with them and tried to bind them in chains, Dionysus trans-
formed them into snow-white doves.

VII.

1. According to Hyginus the snake was sent by Hera to punish
Philoctetes for building the funeral pyre of Heracles (*Fabulae*, 102).

2. *Protos* = first, *laos* = host or army. In *Iliad* II, Protesilaus is
described as having been killed by an unnamed Trojan. An oft-

repeated version of the myth holds that Odysseus was the first to disembark, but threw his shield upon the shore and leapt down onto it, so as not to be the first to touch Trojan soil. This does not appear to derive from any Classical source, and is likely a modern embellishment.

3. According to Pausanias (*Description of Greece*, 4.2.7), the wife of Protesilaus in the *Cypria* was Polydora daughter of Meleager (Argonaut and slayer of the Calydonian Boar). The myth here recounted by Hyginus is probably later. It is not mentioned by Homer, who in *Iliad* II describes how "his wife, her two cheeks torn in wailing, was left in Phylace and his house but half established…"

4. According to Apollodorus, Laodamia stabbed herself to death (*Bibliotheca*, E.3.30).

5. This refers to the Greek raids on the kingdoms surrounding Troy, which in most accounts take place after the initial landing (see next chapter).

6. Cycnus or Cygnus (Latin) literally means "swan".

VIII.

1. This meeting between Achilles and Helen seems to be unique to the *Cypria*. Malcolm Davies suggests that Aphrodite's presence indicates a sexual union, foreshadowing a later myth that the two were wedded in the afterlife (*The Greek Epic Cycle*, 1989, p. 46).

2. The episode of the Greek envoys is problematic, with each source placing it at a different point in the narrative. In the *Cypria* it occurred directly after the landing at Troy and the death of Cycnus, but the *Bibliotheca* places it beforehand, with Odysseus and Menelaus travelling ahead of the main Greek army. Dictys describes two separate diplomatic missions, the second of which I give here. The first delegation, comprising Menelaus, Odysseus and Palamedes, sets off for Troy immediately after Helen's abduction, with the Greeks only mustering at Argos after the diplomatic effort fails. I omitted this segment due to the inconsistencies it would have created, and because there is no suggestion that it appeared in the

Cypria. The second mission occurs after the Greek attacks on the Trojan allies, when Telamonian Ajax captures Polydorus son of Priam, from the Thracian king Polymestor. The Greeks hope to exchange Polydorus for Helen, and when the Trojans refuse he is murdered within view of the walls—one of a number of myths surrounding Priam's youngest son, who is slain by Achilles in the *Iliad* and murdered by Polymestor in Euripides' *Hecuba*. I have thus made some minor abridgements in my translation of this passage, omitting references to Polydorus and the fact that this is not Menelaus and Odysseus' first visit to Troy.

3. This is a slight variation on an incident referred to in *Iliad* XI, when Agamemnon slays Peisander and Hippolochus; "the sons of wise-hearted Antimachus, who on a time in the gathering of the Trojans, when Menelaus had come on an embassage with godlike Odysseus, bade slay him then and there, neither suffer him to return to the Achaeans..."

4. Here is a prime example of Dictys' attempts to "de-mythologise" his account; holding mortals responsible for events commonly attributed to gods, in order to present it as a factual history. With the exception of Medea's flight from Colchis in the company of Jason and the Argonauts, the original versions of these myths all feature Zeus as the perpetrator.

5. Trambelus' mother was the Trojan captive Theaneira (in some versions Hesione), who escaped from Telamon's ship by leaping into the sea.

6. A Greek attack on Skyros is referred to in *Iliad* IX, with Achilles and Patroclus having taken the city of a King Enyeus. This is unusual, as the King of Skyros at the time of the Trojan War was Lycomedes; in Book XIX, Achilles even mentions his son Neoptolemus being reared on Skyros. George Huxley suggests that King Enyeus was dead by this time, and his city inhabited by Dolopian exiles who had revolted against Peleus. Thus, rather than attacking the kingdom of his father-in-law, Achilles was making the island safe for his son (*Iphis and the Dolopians of Skyros*, 1975).

7. "Some relate that Chryseis was taken from Hypoplacian Thebes, and that she had not taken refuge there nor gone there to

sacrifice to Artemis, as the author of the *Cypria* states, but was simply a fellow townswoman of Andromache." (Eustathius, 119. 4)

8. Dictys gives the names of Briseis and Chryseis as Hippodamia and Astynome, respectively. I have reverted to the popular forms to avoid confusion. Note that in the *Iliad* it is Briseis—not Chryseis—who was married to King Eetion.

9. In the original text Ajax here assaults Thrace first, and receives Polydorus, son of Priam, from King Polymestor as one of his terms of surrender (see note 2). Dictys has the attacks on the Trojan allies occur before the envoys go to Troy, but I have switched these events to fit the known chronology of the *Cypria*. Note that a Teuthras was also the stepfather of Telephus; they are separate characters, but confusingly, were both rulers of Mysia.

10. Here Troilus is dispatched rather perfunctorily. With no surviving written sources, our understanding of Troilus' place in the mythology at this early period largely comes from painted pottery; depictions of Troilus and his sister Polyxena fleeing Achilles were a popular decoration, often showing Achilles dragging the boy from his horse by his hair. Later writers added a homosexual element, with Achilles slaying Troilus for rejecting his advances, as well as a prophecy that the city of Troy would not fall if he reached his twentieth year. The famous romance with Cressida, described by Chaucer and Shakespeare, comes from the twelfth-century *Roman de Troie* by French poet Benoît de Sainte-Maure.

11. In Dictys' account it is Telamonian Ajax who drives away the cattle, and there is no mention of them belonging to Aeneas.

12. The son of Jason referred to here is Euneus, whose mother was Queen Hipsipyle of Lemnos. During their quest for the Golden Fleece the Argonauts docked at Lemnos, where the women had been cursed by Aphrodite. Their husbands had abandoned them for Thracian slaves, and were subsequently murdered by the women in revenge. The Argonauts, discovering the island devoid of men, fathered numerous children during their sojourn. By the time of the Trojan War, Euneus has succeeded his mother as king of Lemnos.

13. The capture of Lycaon son of Priam is known only from this retrospective passage in the *Iliad*, when Achilles encounters him on

the battlefield just twelve days after his escape from slavery. Despite Lycaon's pleading Achilles does not take him prisoner a second time, instead slaying him and casting his body into the River Xanthus.

IX.

1. There are multiple versions of Palamedes' death. In most accounts he is stoned to death by the Greek army after being falsely denounced as a traitor by Odysseus, but according to Pausanias, in the *Cypria* he was drowned by Odysseus and Diomedes whilst fishing (*Description of Greece*, 10.31.2). Dictys offers a further variation: Odysseus and Diomedes, pretending to have discovered a cache of gold in a well, lower Palamedes on the end of a rope so he can retrieve it. When he reaches the bottom they remove the rope and stone him to death.

2. The following catalogue is essentially a condensed version of the Trojan Battle Order from *Iliad* II, omitting the Dardanian contingent under Aeneas and the sons of Antenor.

3. In Homer, Sarpedon is the son of Zeus and Laodamia, daughter of Bellerophon. Xanthus was the name of a Lycian river and city. This may be interpreted as 'from Xanthus', or (more likely) as another example of Dictys excising the divine from his history, and using the name as that of Sarpedon's mortal father.

4. Homer does not give the name of Pyraechmes' father, only saying that he came "out of Amydon from the wide-flowing Axius" (*Iliad*, II). Dictys has here supplied the name of the river.

APPENDIX

Fragments of the *Cypria*

I have managed to incorporate most of the surviving quotes and fragments of the *Cypria* into the endnotes for the relevant chapters, but we are left with several where the original placing in the narrative is unclear. These I give below. For a much more detailed examination of the *Cypria* fragments, consult Malcolm Davies' *The Greek Epic Cycle* (Bristol Classical Press, 1989).

"MENELAUS, know that the gods made wine the best thing for mortal man to scatter cares."

—Athenaeus, 35 C

> Probably after the abduction of Helen, spoken by Agamemnon or Nestor.

"SO THEY feasted all day long, taking nothing from their own houses; for Agamemnon, king of men, provided for them."

—Alcidamas, *Contest of Homer and Hesiod*

> Alcidamas (c. 4th century BC) here attributes the quote to Homer, who was sometimes thought to be author of the *Cypria*. Possibly describes the feasting at Tenedos, when Philoctetes is bitten by the serpent.

"I NEVER thought to enrage so terribly the stout heart of Achilles, for very well I loved him."

—Louvre Papyrus

Perhaps spoken by Agamemnon, when he offends Achilles by inviting him late to the feast at Tenedos. The false marriage with Iphigenia is also a possibility, although Achilles' level of involvement in this plot in the *Cypria* is unknown—his wrath in Euripides' play may well be an invention of the playwright.

"THAT it is Zeus who has done this, and brought all these things to pass, you do not like to say; for where fear is, there too is shame."

—Plato, *Euthyphron*

Unclear.

"BY HIM she conceived and bare the Gorgons, fearful monsters who lived in Sarpedon, a rocky island in deep-eddying Oceanus."

—Herodian, *On Peculiar Diction*

Unclear. In Hesiod's *Theogony*, which is roughly contemporary with the *Cypria*, the Gorgons are the children of the sea gods Phorcys and Ceto.

"AGAIN, Stasinus says: 'He is a simple man who kills the father and lets the children live.'"

—Clement of Alexandria, *Stromateis* VII. 2. 19

This quote has been thought to refer to the murder of Astyanax, although this does not occur until Troy falls to the Greeks—well after the *Cypria* is supposed to have ended. It may describe what is to come, in the same way that the *Iliad* occasionally mentions Achilles' impending death, or as Burgess suggests, be evidence that the *Cypria* did not originally end before the events of the *Iliad*, and in fact narrated the entire Trojan War (2003, p. 139). An obscure scholia referring to Polyxena supposedly dying of a wound inflicted by Diomedes and Odysseus during the sack of Troy in the *Cypria* may support this theory, or else be another foreshadowing, as Polyxena is usually depicted as being present at the death of Troilus (see VIII, note 9).

BIBLIOGRAPHY

Source Documents

Anonymous, *Excidium Troiae*, translated by D. M. Smith (2017)

Anonymous, *Dictys Cretensis Ephemeris Belli Trojani*, translated by D. M. Smith (2017)

Apollodorus, *Bibliotheca & Epitome*, translated by Sir James George Frazer (William Heinemann Ltd, 1921)

Colluthus, *The Rape of Helen*, translated by A. W. Mair (William Heinemann Ltd, 1928)

Euripides, *Iphigenia at Aulis*, translated by Edward P. Coleridge (George Bell & Sons, 1891)

Fragments of the *Cypria*, translated by Hugh G. Evelyn-White (William Heinemann Ltd, 1914)

Hesiod, *Fragments,* translated by Hugh G. Evelyn-White (William Heinemann Ltd, 1914)

Homer, *Iliad*, translated by A. T. Murray (William Heinemann Ltd, 1924)

Hyginus, *Fabulae*, translated by D. M. Smith (2017)

Ovid, *Metamorphoses*, translated by Brookes Moore (Cornhill Publishing Co., 1922)

Parthenius of Nicaea, *Erotica Pathemata*, translated by J. M. Edmonds and S. Gaselee (William Heinemann Ltd, 1916)

Pausanias, *Description of Greece*, translated by W. H. S. Jones (William Heinemann Ltd, 1918)

Pindar, *Nemean Ode X*, translated by Dawson W. Turner (George Bell & Sons, 1876)

Proclus, *Chrestomathy*, translated by Hugh G. Evelyn-White (William Heinemann Ltd, 1914)

Reference

Aeschylus, *Prometheus Bound*, translated by Alan H. Sommerstein (Harvard University Press, 2009)

Aeschylus, *The Oresteia*, translated by Robert Fagles (Penguin Books, 1984)

Atwood, E. Bagby, "The Rawlinson Excidium Troie – A Study of Source Problems in Mediaeval Troy Literature", *Speculum* vol. 9, no. 4 (1934)

Atwood, E. Bagby & Virgil K. Whitaker, *Excidium Troiae* (The Mediaeval Academy of America, 1944)

Burgess, Jonathan S., *The Tradition of the Trojan War in Homer and the Epic Cycle* (Johns Hopkins University Press, 2003)

Davies, Malcolm, *The Greek Epic Cycle* (Bristol Classical Press, 1989)

De Sainte-Maure, Benoît, *Roman de Troie,* edited by Léopold Constans (Société des Anciens Textes Français, 1904)

Euripides, *Vol. VIII: Oedipus–Chrysippus & Other Fragments*, translated by Christopher Collard & Martin Cropp (Harvard University Press, 2009)

Euripides, *Helen,* translated by E. P. Coleridge (Random House, 1938)

Flavius Philostratus, *On Heroes,* translated by Ellen Bradshaw Aitken and Jennifer K. Berenson Maclean (Society of Biblical Literature, 2002)

Frazer, R. M. (Jr.), *The Trojan War. The Chronicles of Dictys of Crete and Dares the Phrygian* (Indiana University Press, 1966)

Griffin, Nathaniel Edward, *Dares and Dictys, An Introduction to the Study of Medieval Versions of the Story of Troy* (J. H. Furst Company, 1907)

Griffin, Nathaniel Edward, "The Greek Dictys", *The American Journal of Philology* vol. 29, no. 3 (1900)

Hesiod, *Theogony and Works and Days*, translated by M. L. West (Oxford University Press, 2009)

Homer, *The Odyssey,* translated by A. T. Murray (Harvard

University Press, 1919)

Huxley, George, "Iphis and the Dolopians of Skyros", *Greek, Roman and Byzantine Studies* vol. 16, no. 3 (1975)

Ovid, *Heroides & Amores*, translated by Grant Showerman (Harvard University Press, 1931)

Pausanias, *Description of Greece*, translated by W. H. S. Jones (William Heinemann Ltd, 1918)

Quintus Smyrnaeus, *Posthomerica*, translated by Alan James (Johns Hopkins University Press, 2004)

Sophocles, *Ajax*, translated by David Raeburn (Penguin Books, 2008)

Smith, R. Scott & Stephen M. Trzaskoma, *Apollodorus' Library and Hyginus' Fabulae: Two Handbooks of Greek Mythology* (Hackett Pub. Co., 2007)

Statius, *Achilleid*, translated by J. H. Mozley (William Heinemann Ltd, 1928)

Virgil, *The Aeneid*, translated by C. Day Lewis (Oxford University Press, 1998)

West, Martin L., *Greek Epic Fragments* (Harvard University Press, 2003)

BIBLIOGRAPHY

D. M. Smith is a serial procrastinator and occasional writer and editor. He was born in Hamilton, New Zealand in 1983, and studied Theatre at the University of Waikato. His interests include Greek mythology, all things vintage and antique, English literature, the music of Jethro Tull, tea, and toilet humour. His first novel, *Munley Priory: A Gothic Story* was published in 2016.

He lives in Horotiu, New Zealand with one cat.

Printed in Great Britain
by Amazon

44253797R00112